UNIQUELY NORTH QUABBIN

Uniquely

North Quabbin

glimpses from nine North Central Massachusetts towns
featuring photos by David Brothers • Rick Flematti • Mike Phillips

sponsored by
Athol Savings Bank
North Quabbin Chamber of Commerce
and the cultural councils of
Athol • Orange • New Salem • Wendell

compiled by Marcia Gagliardi
foreword by Mark Wright

Haley's
Athol, Massachusetts

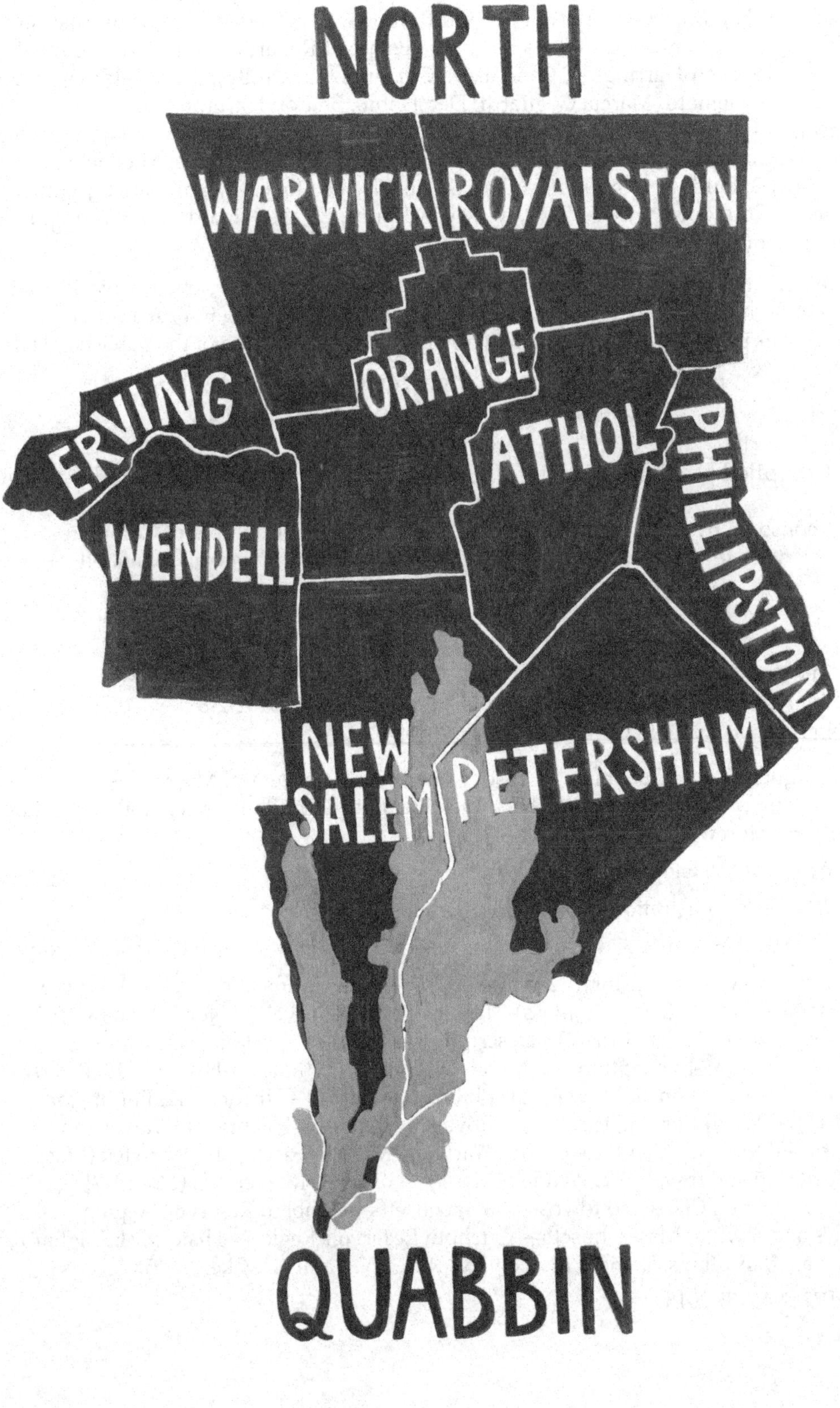

NORTH

WARWICK ROYALSTON

ERVING

ORANGE

ATHOL

PHILLIPSTON

WENDELL

NEW SALEM

PETERSHAM

QUABBIN

map by Casey Williams

Haley's • 488 South Main Street • Athol, MA 01331
haley.antique@verizon.net • 800.215.8805

Compiled by Marcia Gagliardi. Copy edited by Mary-Ann DeVita Palmieri.

Sponsored by Athol Savings Bank and North Quabbin Chamber of Commerce with the Cultural Councils of Athol, Orange, New Salem, and Wendell

massculturalcouncil.org

International Standard Book Number, trade paperback: 978-1-884540-97-4
International Standard Book Number, eBook: 978-0-9916102-2-8
Library of Congress Control Number: 2015943143

Uniquely North Quabbin : glimpses from nine North Central Massachusetts towns / featuring photos by David Brothers, Rick Flematti, Mike Phillips ; compiled by Marcia Gagliardi ; foreword by Mark Wright.

Athol, MA : Haley's, 2015.

260 pages : illustrations (chiefly color), maps ; 25.4 cm

SUMMARY: glimpses of nine Massachusetts towns in the North Quabbin region

1. Athol (Mass.)---History. 2. Athol (Mass.)---Description and travel. 3. Erving (Mass.)---History. 4. Erving (Mass.)---Description and travel. 5. New Salem (Mass.)---History. 6. New Salem (Mass.)---Description and travel. 7. Orange (Mass.)---History. 8. Orange (Mass.)---Description and travel. 9. Petersham (Mass)---History. 10. Petersham (Mass.)---Description and travel. 11. Phillipston (Mass.)---History. 12. Phillipston (Mass.)---Description and travel. 13. Royalston (Mass.)---History. 14. Royalston (Mass.)---Description and travel. 15. Warwick (Mass)---History. 16. Warwick (Mass.)---Description and travel. 17. Wendell (Mass.)---History. 18. Wendell (Mass.)---Description and travel. 19. Cities and towns---Massachusetts---Quabbin Reservoir Region. 20. Cities and towns---Massachusetts---Quabbin Reservoir Region---History. I. Gagliardi, Marcia. II. Brothers, David. III. Flematti, Rick. IV. Phillips, Mike. V. Title.

F72.S94 U55 2015

Contents

Perhaps It's in the Water
   a foreword by Mark Wright, executive director,
   North Quabbin Chamber of Commerce xiii
Birds on a Wire-Less
   Candace R. Curran 1
A Dinosaur's Eye View of the North Quabbin
   an introduction by Marcia Gagliardi 3
Seasonal Images of the North Quabbin and Environs
   a photo essay by David Brothers 6
North Quabbin: What's In a Name?
   Allen Young 25
"Oh, the experience I have had" (Squakheag, 1676)
   Michael Mauri 31
Warwick's Mount Grace 38
Climbing Mount Grace
   bg Thurston 39
The Ellis-Feldman Family and Its Organic Structure
   Susie Feldman 41
The Town and the River
   Robert Collén 47
"I'll Be Seeing You . . . "
   Mary Pat Spaulding 53
Enduring Sports Rivalry
   Athol High vs Mahar Regional of Orange 62
Transplant from Boston, London, San Francisco, and New York
   Connie Pike 67
On the Pulse of a Mountain
   Leigh Youngblood 73
A Special Place
   Pat Larson 79
Something Comforting Dwells Here
   Earle Baldwin 87
Royalston's Two Dam Good
   Kathy Chencharik 93
I Knew I Had Found Home
   Mara Bright 97

Kayaking on Long Pond
  Sharon Harmon 101
A Town Election in Mid-State
  Hugh Field. 102
The Quilt of Praise
  Lynn Dudley 107
On the Road Redux or I Left My Heart in Central Massachusetts
  Jon Chaisson 113
Gone to the Dogs?
  Cynthia Crosson-Harrington 119
To Build a Barn
  Doris Bittenbender with Karl Bittenbender 123
Making Art with a Chainsaw
  Sharon Harmon 131
Polygamy and the Woods at Night in Wendell
  Jonathan von Ranson. 137
Birth of a Legend
  Don Stone 141
Proven Volunteer Support throughout the North Quabbin
  Joe Hawkins 146
Hands across North Quabbin
  Phil Rabinowitz 150
The Village School in Royalston
  Rise Richardson 155
Seeds of Solidarity
  Deb Habib 161
Quabbin Harvest
  Marcia Gagliardi. 165
Johnson Farm's Dede Johnson: General Mills Contest Finalist
  Courtesy of *Athol Daily News* 171
Dinner Theater at Johnson's Farm • Wheeler Avenue, Orange
  Candace R. Curran. 173
Family-Run Adams Farm Slaughterhouse
  Edward Maltby. 175
Television Coverage for the North Quabbin at AOTV
  Carol Courville 177
North Quabbin Newspaper Coverage at *Athol Daily News*
  Deb Porter 183

North Quabbin Radio Station WJDF 184
Beautiful Choral Music from Quabbin Valley Pro Musica
  Mary-Ann DeVita Palmieri. 185
Bursting w/Music: Tool Town Live, Friendly Town Live. . . . .
  Ethan Stone 191
Making a Living by Performing Magic
  Ed the Wizard 193
Honest Weight Artisan Beer
  Sean Nolan and Jay Sullivan. 197
Quabbin Sky Vineyard Makes Wine from New Salem Grapes
  Joyce Wiley 199
This Thing We Call the River Rat Race
  Kathryn Chaisson with David W. Flint. 203
Libraries of the North Quabbin
  Paula J. Botch 208
North Quabbin Shadows
  Phil Zahodiakin 222
Bios of Contributors to *Uniquely North Quabbin* 229

Accompanied by Lester Scafidi and Rise Richardson, top, Millers River Morris Men welcome May at the Village School in Royalston while children celebrate May Day, below. Bill Sullivan of Orange and others learned Morris dancing in Sherborne, England in 1974 and came back to the North Quabbin area to form the Millers River Morris Men.

Millers River, seen in autumn from the South Main Street bridge in Athol, flows some fifty-two miles almost directly east to west from Lake Watatic in Ashburnham through South Royalston, Athol, Orange, and Erving to the Connecticut River in Turners Falls. Nipmuc Indians called the river Paquag or Baquag, meaning "clear water."

Children and adults alike love the fish pond at North Common Meadow, a Trustees of Reservations preserve in Petersham.

Perhaps It's in the Water

a foreword by Mark Wright, executive director
North Quabbin Chamber of Commerce

In all my travels, I've never tasted water from the tap as sweet as I have in my hometown. Others would disagree, many from that very same town. Whether they agree or not, a delicious irony lies in the fact that the town of Athol, like all the towns of the North Quabbin region, receives none of its water from the great lake that has given up its name to us, much like we gave up whole communities to it decades ago. To be sure, some of the water that fills the lost valley makes its way into our wells through the earth, but there is no consideration, nor was there ever one, to fill our glasses with its abundance. So we accept the abundance its creation has given us in other ways.

I'd be happy and honored to tell you about the author if I had thirty or forty pages to do that. I don't, considering that this collection of threads, at once as strong as burlap while delicate as glass, comes from many authors. I'll leave it to you to recognize the patterns of hard work, insight, and joy woven into the pages. The stories are personal. They speak through history, individual enlightenment, and unwavering commitment to our community. Some are blueprints for creating important components of a vibrant successful community. Some could help you create a vibrant self.

I had the good fortune to grow up surrounded by some of these authors. Still others became friends later in life, and we went on to work and play and dream and create together. Many of us still see each other often and continue to dream—and create. There are more dreamers, too. They have already begun to fashion a new life for themselves, the community, and the North Quabbin. With a renewed sense of local purpose and stewardship, they are weaving the new stories for this book.

I'm fairly certain that the region and, most specifically, the Quabbin Reservoir itself, is a lighting rod fashioned from the mettle of the people who surround it. Unique people seem to be drawn to this region, and those unique people create a very impressive energy. There's a spark of that energy in this book. I doubt that those who engineered the Quabbin would have had a natural energy in mind, but while we can't say for sure what may have been without the reservoir's creation, we can reach out and let some of that energy flow back to us from its shores. The natural beauty that fills this entire place is only surpassed by the will and the creativity of the people who call it home.

Perhaps it's in the water.

Spring-fed Tully Pond, seen in winter from Tully Center, a neighborhood of Orange, powered downstream mills well into the twentieth century after it was dammed in the late 1800s to create water power.

photo by Johnny Botch

Royalston's Doane's Falls makes an impressive cascade in springtime.

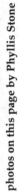

From her Erving living room and dining room windows, Phyllis Stone photographs birds at her feeder, including, clockwise from top, an indigo bunting, a pair of evening grosbeaks, a scarlet tanager, and a red-bellied sapsucker.

Birds on a Wire-less

Candace R. Curran

In rural tradition birds chitchat local
they have their stories they are
authors of a long hand-me-down landscape
members of a competitive glee club
pitching language
somewhat less porch rocker these days
more pool party and lawnmower
sprinkled with backyard warnings they shriek
Nest robber! Cat under the shade tree!
Bear at the feeder!
Others long-winded in field and stream
audition gusty chainsaw they paint the air
wet in brooknotes a tumbling domino effect
they teach native speech and pick-up lines
talk down the nesting sun quieting everyone

At cockcrow a choir of doves whinny off
bursting with sorrow
Urban cousins soar wireless freeways
haunt the altered landscapes
lock their feet on ambiguous signposts
hunting roadkill
Swallow silhouettes crowd and swing like
clothespin birds on a high-wire
Kestrels and crackling black Grackles
ride invisible microwaves faxing from
cell-tower masts tap tap tapping
Faulty navigation!
Magnetic radiation!
An SOS knock-knock-knocking against
deaf ears and thinning shells

photo by Marcia Gagliardi of her mowed meadow

Athol's first 740-acre British land grant to Samuel Morton in 1735 included verdant meadowland behind the eventual Georgian homestead he built with his wife, Esther Goddard Morton. Later, the Lee, Sawyer, and Haley families made the house their home. A 1774 journal refers to the building as a tavern site of Sons of Liberty meetings. State archaeologists estimate that native Americans farmed the land for thousands of years before the British and then Americans usurped it.

A Dinosaur's Eye View of the North Quabbin

an introduction by Marcia Gagliardi

If anyone around here qualifies as a dinosaur, I do. Now in my seventh decade, still surrounded by whatever age-old accoutrements we Haleys and Maronis could preserve, I live and work at Haley's Antiques and Publishing in the eighteenth-century house where I grew up.

Not that I count as the breed of dinosaur with generations of North Quabbin lineage. We Haleys and Maronis arrived in the area late in the day, my father in the 1930s and my mother in 1910. Our Irish and Italian roots got transplanted with countless other immigrant families in the late nineteenth and early twentieth centuries.

My claim to dinosaurhood rests on the simple fact that, despite an affection for big cities and a former and lamentable infatuation with suburbia, I have lived in Athol or Tully in the North Quabbin all my life. I reported for years for the *Athol Daily News,* taught at Athol High School, and served on any number of local boards of directors. During twenty-eight seasons of my proprietorship of Haley's in Athol, innumerable artists, writers, and musicians displayed their work and lingered here.

More than the rest of it, Haley's Antiques and Publishing, my businesses, provide a unique window on the passing scene of the North Quabbin. "The antique business is a great leveler," my mother said often enough to create a mantra. Taking advantage of that unique window, I decided to compile this book about unique features of the North Quabbin. Athol Savings Bank and North Quabbin Chamber of Commerce graciously sponsored this book with the cultural councils of Athol, Orange, New Salem, and Wendell.

Dinosaurhood and a particular view do not constitute my only claim to experience with the North Quabbin vibe. Although no one would call me an athlete (no laughing, AHS '65 classmates), I've taken in many a fine sporting event here. I'm no stranger to locally popular card games: I've played my share of bridge, whist, pitch, and canasta. I've sometimes hung in local bars. I taught Christian Doctrine classes for some years. I played the organ for a decade in the Community Church of North Orange and Tully. My kids grew up here. I love to walk with friends in the North Quabbin woods.

I tell you all this in an earnest effort to establish credentials as one eligible to compile a book called *Uniquely North Quabbin.* In an early twenty-first century way, this book follows in the traditions of histories of North Quabbin towns, of Dick Chaisson's *Hometown Chronicles,* and of Allen Young's *North of Quabbin* and *North of Quabbin Revisited.* We published some of Allen's books here, thanks to his generous mentoring twenty-five years ago when he stepped aside from his own Millers River Publishing Company and taught me the ropes of the publishing game with the help of Ted Chase of the Highland Press and Ted's father Dick Chase.

In this book you will find an array of articles by some thirty participants and observers of the North Quabbin scene as well as photos by authors of this book's articles and several of the region's most capable photographers. I trust you will enjoy reading and viewing the contents of this book.

It pains me that our mill towns, Athol in particular, take the brunt of sick jokes and putdown. It just isn't fair. Not only do natural surroundings enhance our scene. Skilled machinists, builders, mechanics, artists, artisans, laborers, office workers, and entrepreneurs invigorate our landscape and daily lives. Our factories set standards for world industry. Despite our genuine shortcomings, we should take pride in our strengths.

So I present this book to you. It's my own little love song to this stimulating area. I hope you like it.

Greenwich Village watercolorist Ed Schlinski bartered his family's overnight stay in 1956 at Haley's Tourist Home for the painting, top, of the house built by Samuel and Esther Goddard Morton in the mid 1700s. Silas Sawyer added Georgian embellishments around 1810. Mark and Rena Maroni Haley replaced a Victorian porch with porticos in the late 1950s. The barn photo dates from the early 1900s before Works Progress Administration paving of Route 2 (now Route 2A) in 1937, when the barn was moved to the site where from 1953 into the early twenty-first century it housed Haley's Antiques. The house has accommodated more antiques and Haley's Publishing since 1989.

Seasonal Images of the North Quabbin and Environs

a photo essay by David Brothers

Autumn foliage bedecks the Quabbin Reservoir, seen from New Salem.

Crocuses reveal themselves as harbingers of North Quabbin springtime.

photos on these pages by David Brothers

An old stone wall at the Ellis homestead in Athol and rushing waters in Wendell signify spring's arrival.

Springtime greenery decks out New Salem's landscape, both pages.

Athol's Memorial Building, left, and the renowned April River Rat Race on Millers River are found only in the North Quabbin.

A patch of rare red trillium grows on the banks of the Millers.

Tully Mountain and nearby hills undulate over and around Tully Lake.

A monarch butterfly makes a perfect landing on a North Quabbin zinnia.

Royalston's Lawrence Brook flows over Doane's Falls at its last cascade.

photos on these pages by David Brothers

June pinks bloom on Minnie French Conservation Land in Athol.

Millers River tumbles over rocks below Athol's Bears Den.

A Petersham garden blooms, left, miles from the inviting Bridge of Flowers.

Tully Mountain invites hikers to enjoy an easy summer climb.

Warwick sign points to landmarks, left—maybe even to a Hardwick barn.

An old New Salem barn reposes in autumn foliage.

Mystery shrouds Athol and the North Quabbin, seen from Adams Farm.

Enfield Lookout provides a vantage point on colorful Quabbin Reservoir.

Templeton rolls on to South Royalston and Mount Monadnock.

Kayakers take a leisurely paddle on the surface of Long Pond in Royalston.

Petersham gourds and Athol Historical Society show off in fall colors.

photos on these pages by David Brothers

A barn leans in Buckland west of foliage reflections in Millers River.

New Salem's Meetinghouse and Royalston's Spirit Falls bracket the region.

North Quabbin's Tully Pond reposes miles from a Buckland golden maple.

French King Bridge crosses the Connecticut River from Erving to Gill.

Lazy Millers River reflects the sky over Athol.

photos on these pages by David Brothers

Tully Brook gleams, above and below, with snowy, icy splendor.

Athol's Uptown Common and an Athol yard revel in new-fallen snow.

Dark clouds begin to dissipate after a Templeton storm.

photos on these pages by David Brothers

New Salem's Keystone Bridge, left, and an Athol front door channel winter.

An ice storm glazes Red Apple Farm in Phillipston.

Tully Mountain reflects in icy Tully Pond.

Snowy New Salem Common and an icy Royalston tree proclaim winter.

An Athol barn looks festive in winter.

Sap's running and boiling at Johnson's Farm in Orange, left. A touch of snow adorns apples at Red Apple Farm in Phillipston.

North Quabbin: What's In a Name?

Allen Young

Until the 1970s, there was no such place known as the North Quabbin region, but eventually the name became well established as a designation for nine towns in North Central Massachusetts.

The simple name, North Quabbin, as one might surmise, announces that this place is north of the Quabbin Reservoir. And yet, not all who live here think of themselves as living in the North Quabbin. In the rest of the state, the region is not yet well known. I suspect that the majority of the residents of Massachusetts don't know much even about the Quabbin Reservoir itself.

I've thought a lot about the name North Quabbin, and I find it pleasing and useful. The geographic nature of the name is certainly helpful. The meaning of the word "north" is clear to just about everyone, even though I'm amazed at how many people cannot readily point from wherever they are to north, south, east, or west when asked to do so.

The Quabbin Reservoir is surely a well-known feature of the Massachusetts landscape. A quick glance at a map of Massachusetts shows a large lake in center of the state, and that's the Quabbin—though "lake" is not a word usually used for this massive body of water. In addition, there are many people who no longer look at maps and who do not know where their water comes from. There are even more who do not know the dramatic history of the creation of the reservoir!

The name Quabbin for the reservoir was adopted in 1932 in the early days of construction. The official explanation of the name is that the word Quabbin is an approximation of a Nipmuck (Native American) word meaning "place of many waters." A *Wikipedia* page with a "list of place names in New England of aboriginal origin" offers a slightly different translation, saying that Quabbin means "crooked streams."

Before the reservoir's construction, there were two places identified with that name—Quabbin Hill in Enfield and Quabbin Lake in Greenwich. Several websites say that the name comes from a Native American chief called Nani-Quaben. In his 1951 book, *Quabbin: The Lost Valley,* Donald Howe included a poem that refers to "Chief Quabbin."

The reservoir was constructed in the 1930s by damming up the Swift River and emptying the river valley of twenty-five hundred people along with their homes, farms, businesses, churches, town buildings, graves, and trees. Four towns—Dana, Enfield, Greenwich, and Prescott—went out of existence as the result of an act of the Massachusetts legislature. There was limited controversy locally, and the state of Connecticut brought a case before the United States Supreme Court to make sure the impact on the Connecticut River would not be too severe. However, there wasn't the kind of broad grassroots opposition that would happen nowadays.

The reservoir provides water for 2.5 million people in 43 communities, primarily the Boston metropolitan area. Here are a few statistics: reservoir length, 18 miles, reservoir depth, 151 feet maximum and 45 feet average; shoreline length excluding islands, 118 miles; reservoir capacity, 412 billion gallons, top inch when full, 750 million gallons; average daily withdrawal from reservoir by users, 250 million gallons; reservoir surface area, 25,000 acres; watershed area, 81,000 acres.

The history of the reservoir and the four "lost towns" has been the subject of numerous books, and perhaps the best among them is the well-researched *Creation of the Quabbin Reservoir* by J. R. Greene of Athol. The Quabbin watershed has been dubbed "the accidental wilderness," and both the land and the water are open to the public for limited recreational use (with a long list of rules).

Several websites have information about the reservoir, the best one created by the Friends of Quabbin—www.friendsofquabbin.org—at the Quabbin Visitor Center in Belchertown. A museum complex run by the Swift River Valley Historical Society, located in New Salem, is dedicated to the history of the four towns as well as New Salem.

The nine towns of the North Quabbin are Athol, Erving, New Salem, Orange, Petersham, Phillipston, Royalston, Warwick, and Wendell with a total population of about twenty-seven thousand people counted in the 2010 census, up about a thousand from the previous census. Athol and Orange have long served as commercial centers with more than half the region's population residing in those two municipalities. Two of the area towns—Warwick and New Salem—are among the few towns in the state with a population under a thousand. Petersham has the state's third largest area at 68.18 square miles. Only Middleborough and Plymouth are larger. Much of Petersham's territory, however, once belonged to towns that went out of existence when the Quabbin Reservoir was created—and most of that is under water.

The term North Quabbin was first used in the 1970s when Athol Memorial Hospital launched an experimental health maintenance organization or HMO. Hospital officials chose the name North Quabbin Health Plan after consulting with local reporter and historian Dick Chaisson.

The name used for the region at that time by the *Athol Daily News* was Mount Grace Region, chosen by then publisher Edward T. Fairchild. Mount Grace, located in Warwick, is the third highest peak (at 1,617 feet above sea level) in Massachusetts east of the Connecticut River. Several years later, the *Daily News* dropped Mount Grace and declared, as it still does, that it serves "the interests of North Quabbin Region."

The newspaper specifically included nine towns—Athol and Orange with seven towns that border the larger two. Sometimes the newspaper publishes news about Templeton and Barre, but overall, the "nine-town North Quabbin Region" seems to work.

Phone listings include thirteen businesses and nonprofits with the name North Quabbin. One of these is the North Quabbin Chamber of Commerce, formerly known as the Athol-Orange Chamber.

My regional guidebook, published in 1983 and entitled *North of Quabbin,* focuses on the way geography defines this place. The expanded new edition, published by Haley's in 2003, is *North of Quabbin Revisited.*

But while some have embraced the concept of North Quabbin Region for marketing purposes and to promote regional mentality, it doesn't always reflect the reality of the majority of the people who live here. The combined downtown areas of Athol and Orange do not serve effectively as a hub for surrounding smaller towns.

I continue to believe that regionalism and the name North Quabbin remain key to economic growth and community spirit in the nine-town area. More effort is needed to promote the name, the concept, and an awareness of its value. Athol and Orange, in particular, stand to benefit from such a campaign.

It seems to me that the name is here to stay, and with a focus on ecotourism and regionalism, a more likely goal is expansion of its use through a process that has become known as branding. That is a corporate-style jargon that I personally dislike, but I hear it more and more often.

At various meetings I've attended, I have made two suggestions that are supposedly being considered.

One idea is to have highway signs visible upon entering any of the nine towns with the words "Entering the North Quabbin Region." Another idea is to have an organized bus tour of the nine towns for fun and education, starting by offering such a tour to local residents as an experiment. I have developed a route with a few stops, and North Quabbin Trails Association inaugurated Allen Young's Groovy Magical Mystery Bus Tour in June 2015.

Shakespeare's Juliet said, "What's in a name? That which we call a rose by any other name would smell as sweet."

There are some people who don't like the name North Quabbin. Some feel that it takes away from the individuality of towns. Others reject embracing this name because they feel the creation of the Quabbin is a shameful miscarriage of justice, eliminating four towns and causing great emotional and financial distress to the displaced residents.

It has also been suggested that creation of the Quabbin Reservoir harmed this region, blocking access to the part of the state south of here and putting an end to a railroad line that connected Athol to Springfield. On the other hand, businesses from the Swift River Valley, especially some industries from the town of Dana, relocated to the Athol-Orange area, and some people moved here as they were forced out of their homes.

Some people feel that Athol's name is a problem, too, because of a bawdy play on the name. Chaisson wrote a detailed article about this, published in the *Worcester Telegram* March 15, 1987, and reprinted in *The Millers River Reader*, an anthology I published. He explained that the name is Gaelic and means "pleasant place" and is linked to Blair-Atholl and its duke in Scotland. The earliest documented jesting about the name, which never seems to stop, is a 1912 article in a national magazine by a well-known humorist of the day named Elbert Hubbard.

Some have suggested that Athol should go back to the original town name of Pequoig, for the local Native Americans encountered here by the first white settlers. Apparently, the sound of Athol remains jarring for some people, including the developers of the complex around the Market Basket supermarket. The developers started out calling their property Athol Commons and then changed it to North Quabbin Commons.

Athol's problem with its name is similar to that of other Massachusetts towns, including Belchertown, Peabody, and Hyannis.

Here's what I wrote in 1983 in *North of Quabbin*: "Local residents rightfully tend to ignore with disdain the occasional sophomore jesting one hears about the town's name."

The voters of Gay Head, the town on Martha's Vineyard named because of the colorful cliffs when it was incorporated in 1870, voted in 1997 to change the town's name to Aquinnah (and the change was approved by the state legislature). The Wampanoags, Native Americans who dominate the population of this town, claimed this was an ethnic identity issue, but I'm certain it was because the more recent use of the word "gay" was giving townspeople some discomfort.

How does a region get its name? Most regions have a name related to geography, and often the name leaves some wiggle room. For example, the name North Shore can be loosely defined as the coastal area between Boston and New Hampshire, but various agencies in that region define North Shore differently.

As for the North Quabbin, I think the name is sweet, and the region certainly is unique, as will be apparent to anyone reading the rest of this book.

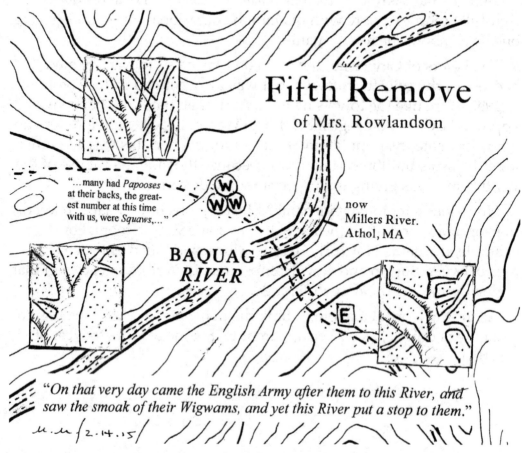

Fifth Remove
of Mrs. Rowlandson

"...many had *Papooses* at their backs, the greatest number at this time with us, were *Squaws*,..."

now
Millers River.
Athol, MA

BAQUAG RIVER

"On that very day came the English Army after them to this River, and saw the smoak of their Wigwams, and yet this River put a stop to them."

In 1676, fifty years before British colonists settled Athol, two thousand Indians and their captives from the vicinity of Lancaster, Massachusetts escaped four hundred pursuing British soldiers by fording the river at the site of what would eventually be the South Athol Road railroad trestle. Among the captives was Mary Rowlandson, whose diary published in 1682 provided her account of her captivity. Michael Mauri commemorates the events in the hand-drawn map above and the accompanying poem, which invokes language usages of the seventeenth century.

"Oh, the experience I have had" (Squakheag, 1676)

Michael Mauri

Mary Rowlandson, in your captivity,
sixth to seventh remove, from Lancaster
to Squakheag you were brought, en route,
no road, through woods, an other-world,
through winter air, past English frontier
—it was early March.

On the run, six months
after Northfield's fall—Squakheag's fall—
worn down, captor
and you, captive, both, anxious to grab
what any could
of abandoned ears
on the frozen ground,
of Indian-corn
or any shocks of wheat,
still there.

"Myself," you wrote, "got two . . .
[though] one [soon]
. . . was stole . . . "

It was late winter, none
had much till one, an Indian,
with raw liver came, a basket full,
of it—a horse had been killed,
and though not an English way,
what was there for you to choose
but "eat it as it was," [plain],
"with the blood
about [your] mouth"
"What . . .
can you eat
[this]?" he asked.
"To the hungry soul," you replied,
"[what] bitter thing [is not]
sweet"[?]

Mary Rowlandson, you were brought
to where the English village had been, and said
"[a] solemn sight . . . it was
to see
[it]
—whole fields of wheat
and Indian corn—
forsaken.

First Squabeag, Squakheag, Heakeg fell, to Mohawk rout,
sack, rage of Iroquois League, then Northfield rose, English-fields,
on this same plain, but soon to Wampanoag torch
and Nipmuc raze, up and down,
the length and breadth of it, then Capt. Beers's failed rescue
raid—oh, murderous ambuscade—this
is where you now found yourself, unkind corn-growing terrain
of bloodshed and flame and bones
in the sand, but you "saw
where English cattle had been,"
though now desolate
and, yet, it—even this—was a comfort to you
in such a state
of mind
and such a comfort it was, you said, and so much did it "take"
you, that, right there, "you could have freely lien down
and died."

But no.

***

Mary Rowlandson, you persevered
exceedingly well,
starvation near, on long removes, sleeping on snow,
even while your daughter, Sarah, six years old, could not; she did
perish
of her musket wound; nothing you could do could provide
the help she need,
by your side, slow to die, no Christian burial, lost eternal rest
in unmarked ground, to you
of this

desolate
wilderness
place.

***

Onward, Mary Rowlandson, in service now
of your Mistress, Sachem's wife, she merciless,
—and your captors in their own distress, winter exodus,
in flight, on foot, in fear not mere
warriors, but all the village, all the nation,
all the children,
the old the sick and everyone,
must trudge must flee must run
from English menace,
must grind through snow, and wet and cold, and eat no food, and bear
all their
earthly things, all lives at risk, all survival at stake,
the English ever nearer.

***

—and in loss of child you share, though not in mutual sympathy, for
your captors, too, in their distress, in mourning, have buried their own
papoose—

***

Mary Rowlandson, you ventured out
remove by remove, in captivity, no choice, ever farther, forest, swamp,
steep hill, Bacquag River and Quinetucket great, led away
—no more English town,
no more cattle ground, just "a nation [unknown]"
your family now gone, scattered, slain,
your house fired, burned down in the attack
on your town—your town
burned to the ground, you, with mere oak leaves must cure
your own musket-ball-wound, where it lodged in your side,
though when you fell
down, you were mocked, but, God-willing, not beaten, or knocked
on the head like common goodwife, she "very big with child,"

she, "having but one week to reckon,"
she, stripped naked and danced around, Indians on all sides,
in snow under stars
"as thick as the trees" as far you could see, "a great company,"
she, a knock on the head, a child in her arms as well,
both into in the fire—but you safe to the side—
this was the center
of the New England Death
Fight
with hatchets; you wrote of your thoughts, on, oh,
just one of many "doleful" days,
around you no other Christian soul, hell-bent
towards great defeat, dreadfull
Christian war machinery
plainly evident, everyone knee-deep
in it, late winter snow,
the world reeling.

***

Mary Rowlandson, what gave spark
in this world,
to you, what solidde spirite in you did dwell
and give
survival,
on your own, and will to continue,
with kindnesses few—was it mounting
rumors of ransom exchange for you, hope of rescue,
your captors mention of restraint
from hatchet knock on your own head, prized Minister's wife,
ransomable, your foot dry
on the raft, while others mid-leg deep
in March water, the handful of wheat you got—the Book
from slain hand taken, the Word, from captor given, psalm and
testament within—your deep confidence
in Him—
and tears shed
to wash Mistress's ashes from your eyes, cruelly kicked
to restore your sight, a single respite
of horseback passage one time, harbored—a wigwam in which to lie

in hard spring rain—while others, naked,
under pelting sky—
a generous sip
of stranger's broth, broth of hoof, hoof of horse, and crumbs
of ground-nut cake?

***

Mary Rowlandson, in your book,
you wrote:

"yet . . . . oh . . . how
hath the Lord preserved me in safety!"

What safety, these kindnesses few
bestowed in that time,
of mayhem
continual at your side,
and still you wrote

"yet . . . . oh . . .
the goodness
of God
to me
and mine!"

***

In the end, Mary Rowlandson,
to Him for Safety your praise you sing, prevail,
for Twenty Pounds ransom exchange,
were save, with husband re-join,
and two children survive, anyway, and pull back in,
from disparate region, and Metacom's head
on Plimoth's pike-pole was hung—King Philip—
slain, in Hobomoke Swamp, and scalp removed, and hands cut off,
drawn & quartered and hung from trees, on display, from town to
town,
throughout the land, fingers chopped off and sold—see
a thrilling curiosity
wife and child sold into West Indies slavery,
he, Massassoit's son,

dead, killed, gone, Wampanoag,
Sachem who once welcomed Pilgrim,
and all Creation now turned, and in place of your Great Country,
English life may now resume,
regain Providential Destiny; how else could
that crushing fist-slam-out-come of Christian end,
of fur-trade, gun-trade, wampum-trade, and deed to land, English
word,
jurist's word, word of claim, legality, Book of Word, Book
of Salvation have worked—not fault of yours, not personal—
on all New England,
with musket-flash and blaze of wigwam flame and stockade, distress
entire,
destruction manifest in land
of Wampanoag, in land
of Nipmuc, Norwottuck,
Naragansett, Pequot, in land of Pocumtuck and Pequoig,
Woronoke, Squakheag, Massachusett,
and Agawam, in land of Mohegan,
—all the people, all
of Southern New England Algonquian—
once and FOR all
scatter and KILL all
a threat, to clear this land,
wipe original claim, kill all, replace
all, with Christian Man and Sovereign Race and distant reign,
and market mind and gain
and speculate,
to end—final—Original World, Ancient Plan,
until: what else could, what other claim did,
remain?

And now all is said and done,
you wrote your book, reported from the scene,
and we cherish your account, look back
to your glimpse inside,
and the English did survive,
and the English way did thrive
to this day,

and of that other world from which you returned, alive, from flight
on lost trail's faintest trace, from low crouch of wigwam smoke
to exit into quick sting of winter night's deep black space,
just this—your—
winding down story
left to tell.

FINIS.

(based on the original narrative by Mary Rowlandson in her 1682
book *The Sovereignty and Goodness of God, Together, With the Faithfulness
of His Promises Displayed; Being a Narrative of the Captivity and
Restauration of Mrs. Mary Rowlandson*, published in *The Sovereignty and
Goodness of God: with Related Documents*, edited by Neal Salisbury, The
Bedford Series in History and Culture, Bedford/St. Martin's, 1997)

*Staging the above photo at the same time of year in the twenty-first
century, Michael Mauri commemorated Mary Rowlandson's 1676 crossing
of Baquag River. Later named the Millers River, the Baquag provided
Rowlandson's two thousand Indian captors and their captives an escape
route from four hundred pursuing British soldiers on March 3, 1676.
Rowlandson's 1682 journal chronicles the events Mauri honors in his
poem, "Oh, the experience I have had."*

Warwick's Little Mount Grace trail provides shade.

Warwick's Mount Grace

At 1,621 feet, Mount Grace is the third highest elevation in Massachusetts, east of the Connecticut River. Recreation activities at the 1,458-acre state forest include hiking, walking, horseback riding, cross-country skiing, snowmobiling, and hunting (in season).

Mount Grace is connected with a famous episode from the era of Colonial skirmishes against the Wompanoag Indians, known as King Phillip's War. In 1676, Mary Rowlandson of Lancaster (a town forty miles to the east) was captured, along with her infant daughter Grace, by a band of King Phillip's warriors. On a march toward Canada the baby died and is said to have been buried by her mother's hands at the foot of the mountain that now bears her name.

— http://www.mass.gov/eea/agencies/dcr/massparks/region-central/mount-grace-state-forest.html

Climbing Mount Grace

bg Thurston

I was sent from myself as a messenger to myself.
And my essence testified to myself by my signs.

—Ibn Al-Farid

My swollen eyes are hooded by sky.
Between these humps of mountains,
the wing-shadows of birds

bright or beaten against the empty air
all around me. Noisy messengers
come from beyond, deliver my signs.

Broken by spring, I wait
to be done with its firsts,
refuse forsythia's blossoms.

Heaven folds back into blue
while below March roars,
melted snow tumbling over stone.

courtesy of **MetroWest Daily News**, *Framingham, Massachusetts 2012*

Ben Feldman, longtime Athol town treasurer, and Margaret Ellis Feldman—horsewoman, artist, and Athol Public Library trustee known by everyone as Susie—exemplify public service and commitment to the North Quabbin. They have protected hundreds of acres of their Athol, Petersham, and Phillipston land from development. Their family history in the North Quabbin extends through many generations. They take the sunshine, above, with their grandson Elliott and Susie's horse, Elke.

The Ellis-Feldman Family and Its Organic Structure

Susie Feldman

I've been listening to the love songs of frogs lately. There are lots of frogs around, but this particular pair intrigues me. The lady frog, or at least the one I imagine is a lady, sits under my deck and issues her sultry call to her beau, who resides in the garden pond across the lawn. When I was a child, here on this same land, my father and I used to sit on a rock by the Frog Bog and listen to the chorus. He'd tell me about how, when he had been a boy, he'd listen to the frogs near the river in what is now downtown Athol. There's an entire chorus of frogs from the woods and the swamp tonight, but the two I am eavesdropping on are distinct, and their conversation rambles on through the evening. It is a small wonder of nature but significant of the peace found here in the North Quabbin area.

Our North Quabbin family is an organic structure, much like a tree. Its roots extend deep into the earth, the trunk is its solid heart, and its branches and leaves depend on external influences. As I sit here (still listening to my frogs) I am in the core of the tree trunk, roots extending back into the centuries, new leaves sprouting for the future. But people are more peripatetic, and the tree serves as a magnet that draws them to its shelter.

My personal history here commences in the 1800s, when the Bates and Ellis families came to Athol to establish businesses and new lives. They grew, intermarried, and used their combined skills to help build the twentieth century industrial town, planting the symbolic tree, sending out its first shoots, and establishing its roots. Great-grandfather George Albert Ellis, back in the day, was one of the civil engineers who designed the Rabbit Run train track that connected several Quabbin towns. He also was half of the Whitcomb and Ellis Coal Company. Meanwhile, the Bates Brothers established their Wallet Shop on the grounds where the parking lot of the new Athol Library now stands.

Albert Nelson Ellis, George's son who was always known as Pete, married the Bates's daughter, Maude Emily, and they lived in a large brown Victorian home that still stands on Ridge Avenue. Albert was on the planning board for the town hall, where his photograph can still be seen still watching over selectmen's meetings and other events.

photo courtesy of Susie Feldman

Bates Brothers Wallet Shop, above, stood on Island Street, Athol, for more than a century until it gave way to a parking lot in 2013.

My late father Richard Ellis was their child. Like youth everywhere, he grew up planning on "getting the heck out of here!" His educational path led him to larger cities in the US and abroad, but after he'd experimented with travel and his urges to become a poet, he found the call of home too strong to resist and moved back, settling in Tully. He had met and married Barbara Sleigh, an artist who had come from a more urban background. He, quite comfortable with local life, taught English at the high school, worked at the Union Twist Drill, went back to teaching mathematics at AHS, and then served as its principal in the 1960s. Barbara's adjustment to living in this rural area was not as easy. She did, however, grow to develop a deep, strong love of the region. Because of her intense devotion to watercolor painting, her connection intensified with every image she created, and the network of people she knew and influenced expanded. She was one of the creators of the Athol Artist's Guild and a leading light of the Petersham Craft Center. Both of these strong, creative people were deeply committed to community and gave back much more than they received by their consistent engagement in the schools, industry, and arts development.

By the time my brother and I came along, our parents had bought a hunting cabin and some forest acreage on the Petersham town line. At that time, the house had no heat, plumbing, or electricity, but it did

Susie's mother, the watercolorist Barbara Sleigh Ellis, rendered the family home on Briggs Road sometime in the 1950s.

have a wonderful view. It was heaven to be a kid there, but I'm sure my mom didn't like cooking on a wood stove in the summer! Meanwhile, much like our dad, I had become convinced as I grew that this North Quabbin area was simply *not* where I wanted to be as an adult, that "real life" was somewhere else. So, off I went to college, jobs, city life, and marriage.

Onward to my husband Ben, who grew up in suburban New Jersey and had every intention of remaining there. Our attachment to the North Quabbin area became deeper as we visited family here over the years, and eventually we moved back with our three young children to a life we felt was more appropriate for all of us.

Ben states that the welcoming, accepting qualities he found here are a dominating factor in his contentment. The roots of family were there to sustain him, admittedly, but he settled right in and was soon an integral part of town management. He became Town Treasurer for many years and still is, although retired, much involved in the town and regional government issues and has become pretty much a local. His commitment to local progress in terms of the food co-operative, citizen advocacy, and forest stewardship is inspiring. We tend to joke about how long it can take to become a native of town, but he's managed to achieve that status by his involvement in the greater good of the population.

So, while we were steadily involved with local organizations and activities, our children grew, feeling their own normal sense of adventure, needing to escape the small-town ambiance for the bigger life that's out there somewhere. They scattered for college and jobs: leaving home, we were sure, forever. However, the lure of the Athol hills proved strong; all three have now returned, with spouses from other regions of the US, and they have chosen to raise their families here. They and their spouses have used their talents to enrich the community as well: they are involved with local schools, libraries, conservation organizations, and creative endeavors. As this generation has become involved in the doings of the towns, the family branches going back to their great-grandparents (or great-grandparents-in-law!) both shelter and inspire them.

Even one of our former exchange students, who had spent his senior year at Athol High school while living with us, has felt the pull of the area and returned to make his new home here.

And the shoots keep coming. There are now youngsters of a new generation growing up. It is probable that they will scatter in their young adulthood, but we hold forth hope that the allure of that ancient tree, gnarled but still strong, will prevail, and those who have not yet arrived will be able to listen to the frogs' love calls.

Early summer flowers festoon the fence in front of ancient trees in the Feldmans' yard.

photo by Marcia Gagliardi

photos by David Brothers

In his poem about Orange, "The Town and the River," Robert Collén ends by referencing the buildings and bridge, above: "The next morning I drive to work across the bridge, / Over the river, past red brick factory buildings / And the peace monument, and through the center of town."

The Town and the River

(the late poet's homage to Orange, Massachusetts, his hometown)

Robert Collén

For Gloria

1.

"A hardscrabble New England mill town with
    decaying factory buildings."
That is one way to describe it, not original,
But the newspaper reporter was in a hurry, passing through,
And wanted a quick impression to hook the reader's attention
And to show solidarity with the working poor.
Who knows? The frisson of recognition might happen.
Satisfied that he had caught the spirit of the place,
If nothing else, he moved on to a more important story.

2.

What he did not see was the river, the way it sweeps into town
With its burden of sky, clouds, sun, moon, stars, birch trees,
Factory buildings, fire station, and neon *Michelob* sign,
Disappears under the bridge, emerges again,
Gathered and concentrated as it approaches the dam,
And then leaps, sparkling, into the imagination,
Where years later the observer can hear the thunder of roiled water.
The river, its power undiminished, flows through dreams, daydreams,
And memories until it finds its way to the ultimate sea.

3.

For as long as I can remember I have stopped to look at birch trees
Growing along the river above and below the dam.
When I was young and romantic, I thought of these trees
As adolescent girls, pursued by an insatiable god,
Who, in the moment of ravishment, changed them
Into ecstatic but rooted forms, and who, deathless and ageless,
Ardently moves among them on summer afternoons.
Now that I am old and romantic, I summon from the past
The memory of my youthful extravagance and exult in
The excessive glory of white birch trees along the river.

4.

Some say the Scotch-Irish settled this town, but I say
Whoever came here looked back to the ancient Greeks
And planted Doric columns in front of the big houses
On West River Street, under the portico of the great mansion,
In the recessed entrance to the library, and on porches of
       lesser houses
On almost every side street to defy the encroaching formlessness,
To resist the temptation to sprawl, to give in, and to forget.
In a magnanimous gesture, a doctor imported marble from Italy
And mounted Ionic columns, entablature, and pediment
Over the entrance to his white two-story frame house
In honor of Asclepius, son of Apollo, god of healing.

5.

Everywhere there is evidence the town remembers her soldiers.
In Central Cemetery, a column rises to those who fell
At Antietam, Chancellorsville, Fredericksburg, and Gettysburg.
On the common, close to the river, the bronze figures of a soldier
And schoolboy commemorate the War to End All Wars.
The motto on the base of the monument reads:
      IT SHALL NOT BE AGAIN.
Streets and crossroads bear the names of the eleven
Young men who did not return.
On the honor roll in the front of the library,
The names of men and women appear alphabetically
Under World War II, Korea, and Vietnam.

6.

Buildings in the center of town look toward the river,
As if in expectation of some arrival, as if Cleopatra's barge might heave
Into view, purple sails unfurled, to the sound of flutes and drums,
Or, as if out of the Orient, a new light might come to restore
To its original state all that has been lost, worn out, and violated.
Standing on the bridge at dawn and facing east,
As the wind shifts and slides over the dark water,
I have often imagined it is June 1914, that the world has not taken
The road to the slaughterhouse of the Somme and Verdun,
And that fire and sword, to use outmoded symbols,

" . . . the bronze figures of a soldier / And schoolboy commemorate the War to End All Wars."

Have not consumed and wasted the blood and treasure of nations.
These are the tears in things.
The barge, we know, will not come, and the past cannot be undone.
The slow work of decay goes on, dry rot gnaws the sills, paint peels,
And broken windows, vandal's havoc, get boarded up.

7.

What is seen sees. The river looks up at us, takes in who we are,
What we do, and, in flowing on, remains what it has always been:
Barrier, frontier, passage, provider of power, dreamer's mirror.
To cross the bridge two, four, or six times a day is to reenact
The great migrations, for rivers stand between today and tomorrow,
Who we are and what we will become. That we are ignorant
Of what we do changes nothing. We, who are never the same,
Cannot cross the same bridge twice. Everything flows
     over and under
The bridge, and the river ceaselessly whispers its secret name.

8.

Walt Whitman, how often have I wished that you could walk with me,
That we would stroll together on South Main Street toward the river,
That it would be July or August, that men in work clothes
And women in summer dresses would wave to us,
     that we would come
To the bridge at sunset and stand, looking west beyond the dam,
Where water tumbles over rocks, turns white, and shimmers,
That the brick factory buildings would flaunt their fantastic shades
     of red,
That you would sing to me in the voice of friend and guide,
"Flow on, river! flow with the flood-tide, and ebb with the ebb-tide!
"Frolic on, crested and scallop-edged waves!
"Gorgeous clouds of the sunset! drench with your splendor me,
     or the men and women generations after me!"
And that you and I, Walt Whitman, would stand alone
On the bridge and wait for night to come.

9.

The four-square Savings Bank faces south and waits for the sun,
An architect's blind tribute to Picasso, Braque, and Mondrian.
I have seen the midday sun transform this cube into
      a burst of gold
So intense that I have had to shield my eyes from
        its reflected fire.
Interest and credit! What are these compared to a moment in the sun?
Do not be concerned about encouraging the useful, Goethe said.
The useful encourages itself. Encourage beauty,
        even if it does not endure.
I wish I had the skill of an old Flemish master to paint
The young woman who, on a sultry summer afternoon, leaned against
The public drinking fountain while she waited for
      the water to run cold.
Twenty centuries of western art concentrated in her stance
And vanished when she walked away.

10.

Sometimes at night I wake to the throbbing of a freight train
As it works up the long grade and sounds its whistle at
      Wendell Depot.
The tracks parallel the river, the white water, and wide reaches
Where the windless surface is broken only by a snag
Or the prow of a sandbar.
And sometimes in that state between
Waking and sleep, long after the train has passed through town,
And the tunnel has filled with the darkest part of night,
I become the river, and what I know in the depths
Are words, images, and metaphors borne on the surface,
Things that are and that are not, the moon and Cleopatra's barge,
The birch trees and the shape-changing god, time and nothing.
It is then that I return to the river what the river has given to me.
The next morning I drive to work across the bridge,
Over the river, past red brick factory buildings
And the peace monument, and through the center of town.

The lines quoted in Stanza 8 are from Walt Whitman's poem, "Crossing Brooklyn Ferry," as published in the final edition of his book Leaves of Grass *(Philadelphia, 1891-1892).*

Mary Pat Spaulding got a special lift during their leave from World War II duties from her soldier brothers, Roger, left, and Seth.

"I'll Be Seeing You . . . "

Mary Pat Spaulding

For more than seventy-five years, despite sometimes visiting or even briefly living in far away places, I have considered the North Quabbin area my home and haven. After high school, my parents saw me off at the Athol depot on a train bound for Arizona and Phoenix College, but I found my way back to Athol. Even following study at the Los Angeles Art Center and being wowed by living in a small house on the ocean in Manhattan Beach, there was always something so sweet about going home. The area is staunch and substantial—and my roots.

Ten months in Europe traveling on a motor scooter certainly provided high adventure for me in 1956. I oohed and ahhed at the best of Michelangelo in Florence, thrilled to Josephine Baker's swan song in Paris, and became acquainted with cheese fondue high in the French Alps.

Certainly it was the trip of a lifetime, but Europe's scars from WWII still then in evidence reminded me of my experience of the war as I grew up in Athol little more than a decade earlier.

Mom once quipped that it seemed she was always waiting for someone or something.

Almost weekly when I was growing up in the 1930s, my father's work took him away from the North Quabbin. During the waiting for Friday when he would return, Mom busied her days with her beloved flower garden or the Why-I-Like-Duz-Soap-in-Twenty-Five-Words contest or making a lighter-than-air lemon sponge pie—until the weekend brought his sedan down Greenwood Terrace and home to us. Dad occasionally produced lobsters or other magic surprises. He was in the adhesives business (Mom playfully called him a "glue drummer"). Oh, what joy when he brought me a pair of skis with experimental plastic bottoms!! Years later, he and I might split a four-pack of Lowenbrau and even have a cigarette in spite of Mom's disapproving arched eyebrow. Also, many years later, I rued the custom.

World War II found a Victory Garden crowding out Mom's hollyhocks and petunias. Our family sent one son off to be a fighter pilot, the other a tail gunner, to battles fought in places that were, indeed, foreign to all of us. As Mom waited for them to return safely, she hung the flag with two stars that graced so many Athol windows

53

to signify sons at war, took a job at the Starrett company (which was tooling essentials to the war effort), and guarded our food ration stamps with her very life. She sent V-Mail to my brothers . . . and tried to be brave. I think she prayed a lot.

My jobs were kneading margarine, flattening tin cans, and bundling newspapers. One evening a week, we both went down to the then First National Bank, climbed the stairs to the rooftop, and searched the evening sky for enemy airplanes. I considered it my patriotic duty to memorize the silhouettes of any foreign plane that might be incoming. It was serious business, and never have I since felt the wave of patriotism that consumed us all to the extent that it did during those frightful years.

As she was at work fitting Part A to Part B at Starrett, the dreaded War Department telegram arrived stating that Roger's fighter plane had been shot down over Germany and he was missing in action. She stood alone outside the factory, waiting for a taxi to take her home. After that news, I can't remember her smiling much for a while. Still, we had to go on.

Another chore of mine was to pick up the daily groceries at Call's Market uptown just below Dick Waterman's hardware store (which also housed a post office branch). Mom phoned in the orders and entrusted to me her precious rationing stamps, which accounted for the rations permitted our family during the war. I loved watching the butchers wrap the items, pull the twine from a ball overhead, bind the package, and finish off by breaking the string against itself. It was as close to ballet as this ten-year-old had ever witnessed. There was always a small radio on the counter playing. One day while I was at Call's, the music was interrupted by a voice saying ". . . and we dedicate the next song to Roger Spaulding." Bing Crosby began to croon "I'll Be Seeing You." Everyone in the entire tiny store listened, intent on every word, as though there might be a clue as to his welfare or fate.

Eager to get this monumental news home, I tore out of the market— forgetting the groceries—and somewhere lost the tokens (change from the food stamps).

My feet barely hit the ground, and I was home before I could have sung two stanzas of "Off We Go into the Wild Blue Yonder." Mom cried, then laughed, cried some more, and I think considered the event a good omen.

photo by Seth Spaulding

Mary Pat fairly flew home to tell her mom she had heard a song dedicated to her brother Roger, missing in action for a time during World War II.

A month later the Red Cross called to say that Russian soldiers had liberated my brother from a German prison camp. The worst waiting ever had ended. The war was nearly over. She began to be happy once more—and, thanks to my lucky stars, she never mentioned nor even once scolded me for the lost food tokens.

My brothers, mere boys just "yesterday" went on to become men who were affectionate husbands, loving fathers, and good citizens who made positive difference in their communities. I still miss them and cherish their dear memories.

Now and then, a beautiful piece of music or lovely work of art has the power to cause almost physical pain, and I cannot hear the sweet melody and lyrics of "I'll Be Seeing You" without being struck by nostalgia.

Artist Ami Fagin of New Salem captures the Crescent Street, Athol, corner dominated by the L. S. Starrett Company, known around the world for its precision tools including micrometers, calipers, and gauges that measure ten-thousandths of an inch or similar tiny fractions of a centimeter. Manufacturing represents a considerable portion of the North Quabbin's economic base.

Athol Hospital, a member of the Heywood Healthcare Family, provides medical services to residents of the North Quabbin.

Athol-Area YMCA offers the area a range of physical fitness opportunities, including an Olympic-sized swimming pool, basketball court, Nautilus, fitness machines, courses at all levels. Community meetings often take place at the Y.

photo by Brandy Lefsyk

Orange's The White Elephant, owned by Connie Pike and Mike Magee, sponsors yoga and other disciplines, as do community programs in most North Quabbin towns. For many years, Nancy and Brian Lagmoniere have cultivated an internationally renowned Tae Kwon Do studio.

Orange Municipal Airport has served the North Quabbin since 1929.

Jumptown Skydiving at Orange Municipal Airport continues the legacy of Parachutes, Inc., founded at the airport in the 1960s by American and French veterans of the 1944 Normandy invasion.

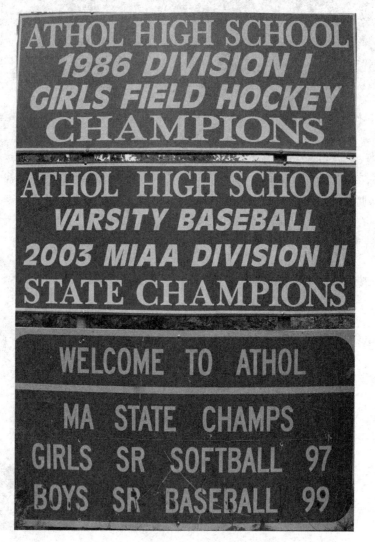

Enduring Sports Rivalry
Athol High vs Mahar Regional of Orange

ATHOL HIGH SCHOOL
1986 DIVISION I
GIRLS FIELD HOCKEY
CHAMPIONS

ATHOL HIGH SCHOOL
VARSITY BASEBALL
2003 MIAA DIVISION II
STATE CHAMPIONS

WELCOME TO ATHOL

MA STATE CHAMPS
GIRLS SR SOFTBALL 97
BOYS SR BASEBALL 99

Brag boards, above, for Athol High Schools major sports achievements stand at Exit 18 from Route 2 to Route 2A. Mahar Regional's brag boards, right, adorn the schoool's front entrance in Orange.

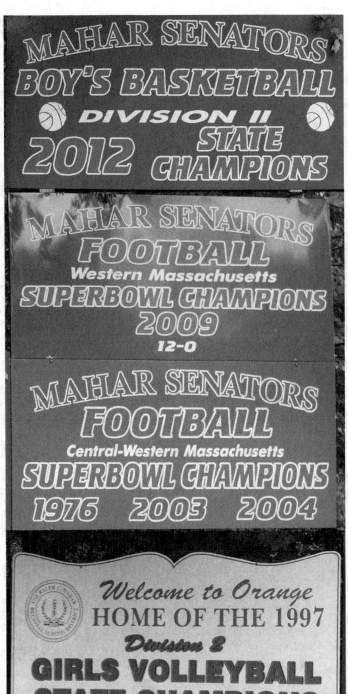

Mahar's Owen Cook attempts the steal, top; Athol's Emily Casella takes control.

photos on these pages by Mike Phillips

Athol's Mindy Martin outreaches an opponent, top, while a Mahar player pursues his Athol opponent.

photo by Connie Pike

Connie Pike and Mike Magee of Orange cultivate the wildness of their North Quabbin land.

Transplant from Boston, London, San Francisco, and New York

Connie Pike

Outside my kitchen window is a poorly groomed hill of early spring with the first of many daffodils in bloom. Beyond the pathetic few, a huge boulder has landed and remained, and beyond it are two upper fields. Rising up behind the fields where cattle used to feed are white pines, some spindly and scrappy, some with lower spiky branches, all in the way of casual passersby. But then there are those trees that become majestic as we come to appreciate what is quintessential to the North Quabbin.

Initially to a transplant like me, the forest is not friendly. It is dark and unkempt. Only when a ray of sun shines through am I able to feel okay. However, one must walk through the forest to see the nests of great blue herons or the black gum swamp or cellar holes of those who bore such hardships to live here long ago. The trees of kinder climes abound as well amongst pines and Frost's birches. To an outsider,especially someone from the city, there are definitely too many trees, but when the hills are aflame, I bless every one.

My life before the North Quabbin was in New York City, San Francisco, Boston, and Oxford, England. Nature to me was Cape Cod's Wellfleet, New York's Morningside and Central parks, San Francisco's Golden Gate Park, Oxford's gardens, and Boston's Arnold Arboretum, where my husband and I met. When my husband-to-be Mike Magee first brought me to this region, his forest appeared messy, unarranged. It tripped one up. One had to bushwhack. Such fun! And there were no labels on the trees as in the parks and arboretums I had frequented.

However, until I truly crossed over or passed through to make our home in this rough and tumble of the North Quabbin, how could I see its infinite majesty? After I moved here and before my life became busy, I walked eighteen miles in the Quabbin Reservoir every week—six miles, three times a week. And, it was always the same walk. Others wondered why. The same was always different, and that was what I longed for. I still miss those walks, but I find the same miracles on my shorter walks on my own land.

For twenty-seven years, two years before I moved here, there has been a community garden on a fifteen-acre parcel of our land down by the Millers River, a river I raft on, walk across, and swim in with my dogs. The Millers River Community Garden was founded by a Roman Catholic priest from Orange to provide room to grow organic vegetables to those who did not have enough of their own. At one time, we had sixty-four gardeners on that land. With my dear friend, the late Dottie Cleveland, we published a monthly newsletter. Mount Grace Land Conservation Trust runs the garden.

Our earliest affiliations in the area were with the Millers River Community Garden, Mount Grace Land Conservation Trust (sixty-five of our acres are in a conservation restriction facilitated by the land trust), and the Millers River Watershed Council. The last has for decades worked diligently to keep our sacred river clean just as the land trust has preserved much land from being developed or clear-cut.

It was an honor to be invited to the board of the Millers River Watershed Council with its founders. Our chair was Rudy Perkins, and we took on fighting the battle against Recontek, a company proposing to build a lead and cadmium processing plant in Orange. A few of us worked constantly, if part time, for two and a half years to oppose Recontek. Not only did we have a blast, but we beat the corporation! On some weekends we gathered to watch marathon showings of the BBC series, *Prime Suspect.*

During the campaign against Recontek, I was fortunate to meet many activists from the town of Wendell and environs, the first town in the United Sates to come out, as a town, against the Vietnam War. This was a town of no more than nine hundred at the time. Wendellites took on the proposed plan to take Route 2 through Wendell State Forest. Those resourceful minds beat the Commonwealth of Massachusetts and derailed the plan. We also met a couple who raised English Springer Spaniels and provided us with our third and very best, Clancey. Their present Springer sired our present Springer, Zinnia, whose nose is a little too pointy and who is a bit of a nervous wreckage at times. But she sure can spring! One of my nearest and dearest friends calls Zin Zin (after Howard Zinn and Jon Kabat-Zinn) "Geraldine McBoing-Boing."

Looking out my window, I have the delight of our own arboretum that we created below the upper fields, much smaller than the one where Mike and I met, but softening the harshness of trees in the forest above. The soil is sandy, and unlike most species, rocks in this region reproduce in the winter. Thus, every spring there are ever more. The

The Pike-Magee upper field shimmers on a mid-winter day.

soil needs culling and feeding and nurturing and mulching—and lots of composted manure. This land is rocky, harsh, and rigid. The people of the North Quabbin can appear the same. It takes a while (or it took me a while) to chip away at that exterior which is just that, an exterior.

In our arboretum, the forsythia and magnolia bloom now. Buds of Chinese and Virginia dogwood are ripe. The lilacs will soon burst. The pseudo-camellia, chionanthus, river birch, Japanese silver bell, sourwood, and tulip poplar all wait to come into leaf. Viburnums will dominate the show when they are ready. Rhododendra will precede them. There are Alaskan weeping cedar, meta sequoia, European weeping larch, and red dwarf buckeye. Though uninvited, aspen and pin cherry intrude. I would rue the day I was reincarnated into a hemlock tree. I wouldn't mind being a river birch or a black cherry. However, were I a white pine, even a scrawny one, I'd always know I was home!

Even in our hardiness zone of Number 5, shrubs and trees actually grow in our arboretum in the Holtshires of Orange, and yet, I never assume they will come back. Actually, I have a true resentment that the North Quabbin lies in Zone 5. Frangiapani and bougainvillea cannot grow here. Even the albizia will not tolerate us. After living in a snowbank for five months a year, what delight at the miracle that beautiful leafy, blossoming creatures return once again, even stronger. How do we manage such winters without drinking ourselves to death? We make it through with a lot of inward glances. That is what our winters are for, to give us that opportunity.

"I'm older than I once was" (Paul Simon) and not so active on boards or committees. The North Quabbin has given me a good living in my two callings as psychotherapist and yoga teacher. As I look back to groups I was involved with, I am very proud to have been part of the North Quabbin Community Coalition in its early days. Its directors have been women outstanding in their vision, activism, and leadership regarding social problems of the area. Yes, there are a lot of social problems here, and as a social worker, I see that daily more than most. Rural areas tend to be poor and without resources. What is unique about the North Quabbin Community Coalition is that it brings disparate people together aggressively and effectively going to bat for the underdog. Its leadership has reached out to one and all, bringing out the best in us so that we can take on the work at hand.

After 9/11, the response for some of us was, "Oh no, the United States will seek retaliation." Some were spurred to immediate action. A weekly silent protest was held on Saturdays in Memorial Park in Orange. We followed the tradition of Women in Black, women in Palestine and Israel who joined together to promote peace in that region. Our goal was to send the message to the American government to stay out of Afghanistan and later Iraq. I stood with the group for most of its five-year tenure.

What is common about the people and groups I have mentioned? Nothing! They are uncommon. I very much doubt that Bob Gray of the Millers River Watershed Council considered himself an environmental activist. He just wanted a clean river so he could fish with his grandchildren. Barbara Corey's path began as a community organizer for North Quabbin Community Coalition, but she became a community activist. Jim Diemand, the priest who started the first organic community garden in the North Quabbin region was no great initiator. He was a pragmatist. He wanted a fertile piece of land where all could have access to clean air and good food and a sense of community. So many people I have met in the North Quabbin simply live the discipline of their belief systems and act accordingly.

When we are younger, we sing to our lovers "When I'm Sixty-Four." Now that we're older, we sing, "When I'm ninety-four." At that time, Mike may not be able to cut and split wood, and certainly I will not be stacking it. What will happen to us in this huge old farmhouse built in 1824? We will look inward and outward. Perhaps we'll buy a used golf cart to travel around and admire the trees. We have the luxury of living on this unkempt and very well kempt land. And, hopefully, we will cross paths with those very special people with whom we have enjoyed so very much while working to preserve and protect the people and the environs of the North Quabbin.

photo by Connie Pike

A vivid North Quabbin sky makes its statement above Connie PIke and Mike Magee's forest in Orange.

A posse from Mount Grace Land Conservation Trust takes in Tully Mountain from Mount Grace's 2007 Gale Farm project.

On the Pulse of a Mountain

Leigh Youngblood

Everything happened here. It feels like the place I came of age, though I was already on the cusp of thirty when I arrived. And it is the place where I found my voice, which first faltered when I was but a small girl. Many have lived long lives anchored by this solid ground. Tully is more than a hamlet situated at the center of the unique North Quabbin. It is a microcosmic confluence of all that I know about land conservation, about the way people and nature can live balanced lives together, and about the *me* I have always been.

Picture a modest monadnock, diminutive by some measures yet distinctive in its singularity of form. Tully Mountain sits colorfully and abruptly apart from the rugged hills in the near distance in every direction. It sits surrounded by cold trout currents of east and west branches of Tully River, bordered on the east by manmade Tully Lake and to the west by the very wild and wide Tully Meadow. The New Hampshire wilderness hosts its headwaters with steep rocky slopes providing cool shade for the water and also preventing too much civilization from encroaching. Everywhere are trees, countless individuals, together blanketing the landscape in alternating shimmers of coppery ice, tints of green, or rich autumn russets.

My workplace was a couple of towns away in New Salem when I first traversed the woods of Tully. William O. Foye, the author, angler, poet, and chemist was ready to donate his second conservation easement along Tully River on the west side of the mountain adjacent to the first easement he conveyed together totaling 219 acres. This conservation project would be my first in my new job with Mount Grace Land Conservation Trust (which those of us who love it call, simply, Mount Grace), a nonprofit formed just eight years earlier in 1986.

Bill Foye grew up in Athol near North Quabbin's cold water streams he would later write about after he went away to college, then became a professor in Boston. Prescient, he began buying land for fish and wildlife habitat in the 1960s, years before it became legally possible to permanently conserve privately-owned land. The tracts he bought in various towns all had one thing in common: they each contained streams good for trout and for fly fishing. As he fished, Bill cast a writer's eye on the flora and fauna he shared the seasons with as he waited patiently for first his father, then his friends and his son Owen to also learn the ways of trout.

I remember my boss and mentor Keith Ross handing me a manila file folder saying, "Just do this conservation easement like the other one from 1990." Armed with a few reference books, the earlier documents, and an adult student's determination to carve a career from my burgeoning education, I did just what Keith advised. Really, the land did most of the work. Ecology is an inherently efficient workhorse. All I needed to do was describe the important jobs the land was accomplishing for the good of the public, and Bill would get a tax deduction in exchange for keeping the land free from development that could undermine the water and air filtering and the soil and biodiversity building that went on twenty-four/seven in his fields, forests, and wetlands.

I was then in my second semester at the University Without Walls, UMass Amherst, a program designed for adults like me with some combination of work experience and enough old college credits to combine into a field of study often of unique design. After seven years working to defend wetlands from people determined to build as near to or as much of as possible, I sought out an education that would enable me to work with a different set of property owners to help them protect land they had come to love and didn't want to see lost to development.

That's what land trusts do. When Roy Wetmore died at the age of ninety-nine owning a thousand acres of land, his wife Marjorie inherited it all. When Marjorie passed away childless not many years later, in 1997, Roy's nephew Massachusetts State Senator Robert Wetmore contacted Keith Ross, who by then served on the Mount Grace board of directors and was employed by the New England Forestry Foundation (NEFF). Roy had bought and sold land and timber his whole life, but not for development. His attorney, the genteel Rand Haven, told me he'd been representing Roy for twenty-five years and that Rand's father had represented Roy for thirty-five years before that. Roy was apparently a real rural character with his own ways. Often on a Sunday when he wanted to talk about his land and timber enterprises, he would simply pull into the driveway of Rand and Edna's house and honk the horn, meaning it was time for Rand to take a drive with him.

Part of Roy Wetmore's dispersed thousand acres was a 330-acre tract on and around Tully Mountain, pretty much but not entirely encompassing the whole mountain. Roy had patched numerous parcels together over the decades. Recognizing an opportunity not to be lost, Mount Grace put down a $160,000 non-refundable deposit to buy all of the land for conservation. That figure was the amount of estate taxes owed upon Marjorie's death. All of the various parcels of Wetmore land in numerous towns together were estimated to be worth a million dollars. So I signed a purchase and sale agreement on behalf of Mount Grace in that amount using our credit line and all of our cash reserves to make the deposit. It was and felt like a huge undertaking for a little land trust with two part-time staffers, but at the same time it was something we knew we must do. Tully Mountain had long been a much beloved local landmark with a well-used network of trails.

Land trusts "find money" to make conservation happen by matching particular natural resources of a property with priorities of a funding source, like a state conservation agency, for example. The 330-acre Tully Mountain tract is a large block of intact, pristine wildlife habitat, the kind of land that MassWildlife might purchase to create a state wildlife management area. I had learned, with trial, error, and advice, that Massachusetts land acquisition processes were competitive and limited by annual budget constraints and timelines. Mount Grace was concerned about getting our deposit back as fast as possible while working on getting the rest of the acres in the estate protected, among other projects. Happily, thanks to a vivid, grant-funded Wildlife Habitat Inventory prepared by wildlife biologist Sara Greismer the winter before Marjorie's passing, Mount Grace was able to buy and sell the land to MassWildlife in three months' time, something of a record in the oftentimes drawn-out state process.

The real estate paperwork side of conservation can sometimes be as much of an adventure as walking the land now and then discovering uncommon features such as bobcat dens or endangered salamanders. When a survey was completed of Roy's Tully Mountain tract, the acreage went from the 283 acres on the property tax bill to the 330 acres we ended up paying for. Of course this meant we had to pay more. You know you are out in the country when nearly 50 acres of land is simply overlooked. In contrast, I own a house in Greenfield that sits on eight-tenths of one acre and has very visible iron pins in each corner. I suspect Roy knew he had more land than he was being taxed for but didn't have reason to prove that to anyone while he continued to own the land.

By this time, I had had my graduation day from the University Without Walls program. After trying to avoid it, another major event in my personal life was unfolding as my second husband and I went through the process of divorce. I found myself in my mid-thirties again a single mother with three sons, now teenagers, from my first marriage. The challenges of my life reached a surreal pitch one Saturday when I spoke with their father on the phone for the first time in twelve years and, then, when later the same day Sara Greisemer stopped by the New Salem cottage-office of Mount Grace to drop off copies of the bound habitat inventory of Tully Mountain along with an impressive array of accompanying photo slides. While I was very much physically in one place, the bones of the past had crossed a vast bridge of time to arrive unexpectedly. They lay revealed and turning inside of me with tangible emotional presence. Thanks to an inherited quality of determination and buoyed by an affinity with nature and the busy-ness of my responsibilities at work, I was able to remain focused and persevere.

I'd spent most of my childhood, into adolescence, a ways downstream very close to the Connecticut River in Springfield, Massachusetts. While I was in early elementary school, Interstate 91 was constructed about a block from my grandmother's three-family house. It is utterly amazing how elevated highways can blend into one's surroundings–sort of. Always a country girl at heart, I found the abundance of inner-city pavement and sparseness of natural beauty not at all nurturing. Very fortunately, my grandmother and grandfather, before his death from lung-cancer when I was twelve, always grew an abundant, organic Victory Garden. We had the only double lot in our North End neighborhood, and every year it produced a bounty of tomatoes, watermelon, peppers, eggplant, and such that got made into delicious home-cooked meals or put up into canning jars in the pantry or gifted to neighbors. We lived modest, working-class lives in the inner city still very much loving the land and nature and always noticing its seasonal influences on our daily lives. One favorite intergenerational pastime was sleeping on the second-floor screened porch in summer in the boughs of the street-side maples.

Waters of the Tully River join the Millers River which flows into the Connecticut and then courses broadly between Springfield and West Springfield on its way to the Atlantic Ocean. Changing surroundings affect water quality to the point of it being nearly unrecognizable as the same water just an hour or so away. At the age of fifteen, I could no longer bear the stark harshness of city life. Traffic and noise are nonstop. Sharing space on the city bus with insensitive strangers on the way to and from my downtown high school became more alienating. It seemed learning was less of a priority than posturing among my schoolmates. Yearning for the natural world, I'd just walk out of school, my steps lightening as I headed down the State Street hill and over Memorial Bridge hitchhiking my way to Agawam where I kept the horse I'd bought with wages from a string of menial jobs.

If you go to work or horseback riding often enough instead of to school, there is no making up the amount of missed schoolwork that accumulates. For that and other more disquieting reasons, I left the tenth grade and Springfield behind by taking a Greyhound bus to Texas with a long-haired cowboy. One thing led to another, and I had soon settled into an eclectic version of family life and college. At the age of seventeen, by the time my high school class graduated, I gave birth to my first son and received an associate degree from a Florida business school. Eventually we traveled back to Massachusetts where our next two sons were born. Adventure continued until the father of this family of five rode off into the sunset without leaving a forwarding address.

Circumstance, love for my children, and resourcefulness guided me first to regulatory wetland protection work and then to a career in voluntary land conservation. Circumstance, love of the land, and resourcefulness led me to say yes when in the fall of 2000 then Massachusetts Secretary of Environmental Affairs Bob Durand met with me at Ralph Longg's Restaurant on Main Street in Athol to say he wanted a land trust partner to lead a five-to-fifteen-million-dollar conservation initiative. It would later become known as the Tully Valley Private Forestland Initiative. At the time, Mount Grace was still a small land trust with only two staff, but we had earned a strong reputation by agreeing to lead a regional conservation partnership in 1997 at the behest of Harvard Forest and the Massachusetts Division of Forests and Parks. A sportsman and longtime conservation advocate in the Massachusetts House and Senate, Secretary Durand saw conservation opportunity when he stood atop the Jacob's Hill ridge in Royalston and looked across the unfragmented forest of the upper Tully River Watershed.

With grant funds, Mount Grace doubled its staff from two to four and proceeded to complete ninety state-funded land deals in the next two years. With the additional work of Keith Ross at NEFF, we spent a total of nine million dollars, helping 104 landowners permanently protect an amazing nine thousand acres in the four-town Tully River Watershed. Almost all of the projects utilized conservation easements, and so the land remains in private ownership and protected to this day. How exciting it was to be able to say yes to every landowner in the region interested in conservation without the usual challenge of finding the money. On a cold December morning, when the project was winding down and Durand was preparing to leave office, an inscribed rock was placed at Tully Meadow to commemorate this unparalleled conservation accomplishment. You will find the North Quabbin Bioreserve Boulder near the sign for the now-twelve-hundred-acre Tully Mountain Wildlife Management Area on Tully Road in Orange.

In the midst of the Tully Initiative, Mount Grace moved its headquarters from the cottage in New Salem to the former Willis Farm house on Old Keene Road in Athol, a location which seemingly appropriately placed our office in the Tully River Watershed. One of many gracious benefactors, Peggy Biggs, who hailed from nearby Greenfield yet traveled the world with her husband, the renowned organist E. Power-Biggs, bequeathed the forty-acre conserved property, restored farmhouse, and stonewall-lined open fields she named Skyfields to Mount Grace because she favored local conservation. It was very gratifying to me that from her sophisticated perspective Peggy valued a down-to-earth approach to conservation. I've found frequently in the twenty years I've worked on conservation in the greater North Quabbin that, no matter their economic position, people connected to this region greatly value its rustic, even rough, rural charm. This modest but surprisingly intact landscape and the combined community of old families and appreciative newcomers here share an authenticity that feels uniquely North Quabbin.

This essay was inspired by the life, writings, and recent passing of Maya Angelou.

Literacy Project teacher Pat Larson, left, and another gardener enjoyed the abundant 1995 harvest of Orange's Millers River Community Garden.

A Special Place

Pat Larson

"Be careful, you may fall in love with this place," the person working in the community development office for the town of Orange said as I left town hall one day almost twenty-five years ago. Often as I walk across the Millers River Bridge in Orange, I remember that comment and how over the years I did fall in love with this place.

This *place*–what is it? Over the past twenty-five years this region has become many things to me. It is not just the geography of place but also the people and diverse landscape of old industrial plants and farms blended with new enterprises. The contrast of changing seasons, changing terrain, and changing land uses contributes to the spirit and uniqueness of this place. The variety of land uses–forests, farms, and industry–blend together and form a mosaic of people and landscapes.

Trying to find one place that is unique is a challenge with so many special places. Recently I returned to an old spot I knew well years ago. The spot is close to the river that runs through several towns in the area. Prize fishing spots stand next to unused and -used factories along the riverbanks in some places. Old foundations indicate small factories of the past while in other spots factories still stand and use waterpower from the Millers River. Other river spots are wooded with trails leading to places where cardinal flowers bloom in summer and ice formations stand like statues in winter.

In one place I returned to after many years, an open meadow stood back a bit from the banks of the river. The morning mist slowly lifted from the meadow area that stood between the river and Route 2. It is a quiet place in the early morning where deer might nibble at young plants. I did not stand in the grassy part of the meadow but in a plowed open field divided into many plots for a community garden. Almost twenty years ago, I came with others to this special place almost every day in the summer.

An older gentleman I knew from classes at the adult education center told me that he came to this spot in the early morning to hoe one garden plot that many people shared. On some mornings the mist blanketed the landscape and deer could be seen wandering across the field toward the forested area on the riverbank. He told me one day, "I stay until the sun rises in the sky and the mist burns off. Then I put my hoe in my old car and leave for the day. But on summer days I return again each morning."

Remembering this gentleman's observations, I thought about how one place along the river became important in my work as an educator. One spring morning while I readied to teach adults and teens in a basement center next to the courthouse, a woman came early to class. I knew that she was excited about something. In the few moments before the start of class, the woman explained, "I know of a project that we could do. We could plant vegetables at the community garden." I think that she knew I might be interested, as I often looked for hands-on projects people could do. We talked that day with other women in class about growing vegetables in a vibrant community garden by the river.

The women thought we should try to grow vegetables. So one day in May, I brought garden tools to the center. Toward the end of class, six women of varying ages agreed to make the five-minute trip to the plowed land by the river. Once at the gardens, we found our designated twenty-by-twenty-foot plot that would be a shared growing space for the summer. There were many other plots, and we discovered that we could learn a lot from other gardeners. In that first year of working with adult students to grow vegetables, we started with tomato plants, bush beans, green peppers, leaf lettuce, zucchini, and a few other easy-to-grow vegetables. As summer passed into early fall, we harvested vegetables that people could take home for their families.

For at least five seasons, people worked to plant and grow vegetables together. Some springs people started seeds inside at the center under lights. People worked together to plan out a garden plot tying all this together with reading, writing, and math. Then when the weather warmed, we started our trips to the plowed and laid-out plots next to the river. Over the seasons, students of all ages participated. Some adults moved on quickly once they earned GEDs while others remained involved in the garden for a few seasons. One season a teen who had recently moved from a large city to Orange commented about broccoli, never realizing how it grew in fertile soil and formed heads. In her mind a person just went to the store and bought it ready to cook. In that moment, she was excited by such a realization. Such moments remained with me as I continued to learn more about using place and our surroundings as grounding for my work as an educator.

Visiting this piece of land when garden plots opened for the spring, I realized how this one spot continued to be an important part of our landscape. The continuing mosaic of people and landscapes woven together create a uniqueness. I think I learned years ago that many traditions and new endeavors help shape the compassion, nature, and spirit of all that makes up this region.

For five seasons, Millers River Community Garden flourished in Orange.

New Salem and Petersham's 'Temperate Eden'

A great blue heron takes itself airborne one July morning near Quabbin Reservoir Gate 29-5.

photos on these pages by Rick Flematti

As summer turns to autumn one September day, a mother bear and her cub saunter across a New Salem meadow soon before the cub would go off on its own.

Just at first light on a September morning at Quabbin Reservoir Gate 29, otters make their appearance.

Male and female hooded mergansers peddle along the surface of Athol's Silver Lake on a November day.

A black-capped chickadee, sharing the honors of Massachusetts state bird with the wild turkey, perches on a winter branch.

Something Comforting Dwells Here

Earle Baldwin

Humankind is molded by immediate environment. In 1969, Peter Corbin, PhD, School of Geography at Queen Mary University of London, introduced that premise to me. Most other things I was taught have proved to have been adulterated at best, but Corbin's point has stayed valid.

The Mount Grace or North of Quabbin region is strong within us, but it may be more correct to state that we live at the confluence of the Worcester and Monadnock plateaus. I have witnessed it to be a temperate Eden. Many writings exist depicting people in our wilds. I choose a different approach. I wish to focus a bit more on our surroundings within us. I wish the reader to summon experiences from within.

We often experience wonder and simply do not notice because it is abundant around us here. We experience this together. We live in a large cohesive community of active, socially adept folks reaching out to each other throughout this region. They are diverse, industrious, active, and political. Here's an observation from a friend in Rhode Island to demonstrate the point: "I drove through Athol, Massachusetts once. Almost every car had a kayak or canoe on top." He was struck by the impact of this wet plateau on residents. Not all people living here are impacted by surrounding life. A portion of every community chooses to isolate itself. Please excuse me as I exclude those folks from our view. One can live in an area and not really understand what is across the street. One doesn't know that Athol's Mary Adams can show you a bluebird at her home most days of the year. One doesn't know that Warwick's Sandy Mallet can show you the once plentiful evening grosbeak. These birds rival tropical birds in beauty. Often we read about activists in our area showing folks places to hike, butterflies to see, ancient bog plants to photograph, or wet places to fish. Mary and Sandy did not go looking. These women are not noted adventurers. The rugged wilds came to visit.

That is the point. Small ancient mountains stand on our horizons. Wild wily rivers thrill us riffling through our towns. Black bear rip open our bird feeders like peanut shells and inhale the contents. Moose stand in headlights on Route 2. Lady's-slippers softly bloom in dark fragrant rich soils. Waterfalls thrill and isolate us from civilized noise. Quiet solitude echoes on meadow paths within populated areas. Our weather is hard on us. Southeast-Asia-style steamy heat crushes our August. Subzero arctic blasts shock our deep winter. Ice storms take down entire forests. Leaves ignite in colors exploding the imagination in autumn. Springs of a thousand greens quiet our winter dread as amphibians, birds, insects, and mammals chorus even through the receding night.

Rivers flood despite two federal flood control dams erected to prevent complete inundation. Raw wind violence occurs in all seasons. Lava-nurtured basalt supports us. Glacier-deposited rocks litter our land like rough toys left behind by untidy giants. Soils crushed, ground, and spread by glacier melt feed our explosion of growth each year. The Athol Fault, a remnant of Earth's spasm as Pangea tried to break apart, is visible on Route 2. We almost floated away from North America long before Africa pulled free to drift towards its present mooring.

Tourmaline and iron are under Warwick. Flint on the mountain in Athol. Beryl in Royalston. Mineral waters were bottled and shipped by steam train from South Athol. The fertile earth of Petersham, Orange, New Salem, and Wendell feeds us. The rivers inundated to nourish our meadows. American Indians and more recent farmers planted lush crops and harbored animals. Still the nutrients nourish us.

Glaciers dropped crushed nutrients from Canada on our lands. Those crushed rocks clean the rain as it sinks into the subterranean fresh-water aquifer below us. This subterranean lake slakes our thirst. We are not new at love of life and Earth. Hundreds of miles of aging, worn paths guide us through property conserved by generations before us. Those clear-thinking elders knew that water was a fragile gift. They protected it. Life was within them.

Once the recipient of every toilet flush in the region, our restored river is now cleansed by mussels. These bivalves filter the cascading oxygenated waters. Most river communities poisoned their aquatic guardians long ago. This plateau fought back well before clean water or clear air was of interest to the money-addicted and power-deluded.

When Boston needed drinking water, Bostonians did not tap into their potent Charles River that runs right through their city. They bullied the four towns of what is now the Quabbin Reservoir. They thieved land, home, and business of four complete legal municipalities. They dammed the minor waters of the Swift River to occupy what they were too lazy to create. They formed a quasi legal governing agency under the aegis of the Commonwealth of Massachusetts to oversee the occupation. None of that reflects respect and understanding of the stewardship required to keep life. Local wisdom was ridiculed and overwhelmed.

Our region instilled feelings of independence, stewardship, and self reliance. Liberty was fostered. The adulterated environment of Boston encouraged a parasitic, elitist, and entitled hierarchy. The majority of "educated" people in Boston still have no idea where their tap connects. Our environment forces us to take responsibility for our own survival. If we spoil our community, poison our air, or pollute the waters, no one will change our diaper and toss it elsewhere. We have learned to band together in governing meetings to work it out. We have learned to appreciate—even cherish—these lands we cannot remake.

The number of selfless people meeting monthly throughout the Mount Grace region to preserve our Eden is fascinating to activists. The water runs through us. The air fills us. Life surrounds and awakens us. Our surroundings school and pleasure us. Young women and men grab fishing poles and catch trout, bass, and pout. Anglers stand in the rivers and brooks gently landing "fly" while hunting brook trout. Guided groups enter our region searching for butterflies of colors and textures unimagined. A carnivorous butterfly survives here. Camouflaged locals pursue abundant American turkey with arrows.

Carloads of driven folks pursue birds in our diverse habitats. Equestrians dreamily ride as one on horses as miles of hidden trail pass below. Bass boats ride the glass surfaces of Mattawa, Tully, and Ellis. Boats fish tranquil Eagleville and Rohunta. Kayaks probe our shallows, and canoes plough our rivers. Bogs steam around rare pitcher plant, sundew, elfin, and boghaunter. Avid hikers log thousands of paces never seeing pavement or telephone pole. Communing to support our wilds, dragonfly chasers sit with anglers at overfilled halls for supper. Land preservationists plan survival of a prairie-like golf course with duffers. We did not create this environment; we were molded by it. For trap-shooter and kayaker it is an addiction. For jogger and picnicker, it is relief. For deer hunter and photographer, the region is home. Skywatchers sip coffee with gardeners at coffee shops. Every town has at least one acceptable swimming place.

A young gas station attendant points overhead to turkey vultures. The Cape Cod resident driving the car authored a book on dragonflies, is a guide for bird watching, and photographed Antarctic birds. The gas jockey with abundant face-piercings saw the Audubon decal on the dragonfly expert's window and assumed he would be interested in the turkey vulture. Says the dragonfly expert, "It has to be in the water!" Yes. In the air, in the ground, and in the water. We have been forged to share, to get along, and finally to support each other.

Our classic New England plateau has formed each generation. The weather, the water, the Earth itself educates and shepherds us. We share our resources with startlingly familiar wildlife. We plant beauty in our land every spring. Our front yards blossom in color all summer. Our evergreens are colorfully lit when the darkest, longest nights fall on us.

Dehumidifiers and sump pumps dry our warming cellars. Humidifiers soften our air in arid arctic nights. Snow shovels are always handy. Lawnmowers are readied in the autumn. Stored food and water ready our response to storm. We keep an eye on our neighbors in threatening weather.

On this northern Massachusetts plateau, our natural surroundings, our familiar environment has schooled and raised us. We have it deep within us. It is life within us.

Peter Corbin introduced me to the assumption that geography and geology are paramount in all aspects of life in humans. As a kid, I was pretty sure he was wrong. I thought we were above it all. I regret that I lost track of Doctor Corbin. His brief teaching tenure in the United States was a gift to me.

Every locality on Earth molds and motivates the inhabitants. I have seen it. My home fosters a people I enjoy, take comfort with, and respect. The future is promising for those who can stand against the wind and know they can survive it. When a kid sporting ornamental metal piercings can communicate helpfully with an accomplished authority from "away," something comforting dwells here.

A hummingbird feeds on a North Quabbin domestic azalea.

photo by Rick Flematti

Roiling white spring runoff flows into containment above Royalston's Birch Hill Dam.

Royalston's Two Dam Good

Kathy Chencharik

"It was Depression days," recalled Leslie Burgess. "You walked for a mile to earn a quarter so you'd have something to put in your belly so it wouldn't shrink up on you."

On March 31, 1933 in the heart of the Depression, President Franklin D. Roosevelt authorized a bill called the Civilian Conservation and Reforestation Act. The Civilian Conservation Corps, sometimes referred to as the CCC or three Cs, resulted. The CCC provided jobs for young men on federal conservation projects. Leslie Burgess was one of these young men. Leslie was a member of the Tewksbury Fire Department at the time, and the fire chief asked Leslie if he wanted a job in the three Cs.

Leslie agreed, and through the chief, he became a member of the Civilian Conservation Corps.

The reference point for the three Cs was in Lowell. Leslie and others were processed through Fort Devens. From there they were split up and sent to different places.

"I landed up here in Royalston," Leslie recalled. "I still don't know how we got up here. Could be an army truck, you know. A whole troop of us. And from there we started work."

They set up camp, consisting of three living barracks with bunks, a hospital, mess hall, and maintenance shop. They chopped brush, laid out roads, hauled gravel, and fought forest fires. When finished with one road, they started another. The roads eventually led into what became known as the Birch Hill Wildlife Management area, run by the Army Corps of Engineers.

A flood in the spring of 1936 and a September hurricane in 1938 caused havoc in the Royalston, Orange, and Athol areas. As a result, in order to prevent a repeat of the past, the Army Corps of Engineers built two dams. Birch Hill Dam, named for a hill nearby, was one of the first dams built specifically for flood control and not water power in New England. Located on the Millers River in South Royalston, it was completed in 1941 and went into operation in January 1942. Burgess, once a manager at Barre Falls Dam, eventually worked at Birch Hill Dam from 1951-1968. He enjoyed making small things with wood. He cut out and sanded little pieces of wood to build what he called a Corps Castle, the Corps of Engineers trade mark.

Jim Bacon was twenty-two-years old when he started at Birch Hill Dam in 1970. He was considered the youngest manager in the country for the Corps of Engineers as flood control projects go when he replaced Walt Divoll as manager. Jim had a high school diploma when he began at the dam, but over the thirty-or-so years he worked for the federal government, he attended different schools and many training sessions. He and his family resided in the house at the dam for many of those years.

"Birch Hill is in Winchendon, Royalston, and Templeton," Jim said. "Near Priest Brook by the Winchendon Fish and Game Club, you'll see a concrete structure that's square and tall. It's a United States Geological Survey or a USGS gauge. There is also one on Millers River near the Winchendon Waste Water Treatment Plant and one in South Royalston just beyond Pete & Henry's Café. All those USGS gauges were in existence before the dam was built. In order to know how much water might happen in the event we did have any significant flood, all that information was gathered and was part of the original design plan for Birch Hill Dam. Like the flooding that occurred in 1936 and 1938, we had a very similar event in April 1987 that was based on precipitation. Snowmelt had just finished, and it rained for a week. The ground was saturated. If the dam had not been here, there would have been flooding again in the South Royalston, Athol, Orange, and Erving areas, all downstream of the dam. Over the years, the dam has been here, it has had about a five-time payback and was money well spent."

A paved road to the dam is a great place to walk, bike, or rollerblade, especially when the gate is closed to traffic. Miles of dirt roads, leading to Lake Dennison and built by the CCC, are also good for walking, mountain biking or horseback riding. And in the woods, you may come across concrete pillars left from the old CCC camps. King Phillip Rock and Beaver Pond are two well-known places to see. A place to launch a canoe or kayak into the Millers River will soon be added to the area. During the winter months, the Birch Hill area is a fun place to snowmobile, cross-country ski, or snowshoe.

On the other side of town on Route 32 is Tully Dam, also run by the Army Corps of Engineers. It is located on the east branch of the Tully River and was completed in 1949. There has been a lake behind the dam

Tully Dam holds back beautiful Tully Lake, a favorite North Quabbin spot for camping and water sports.

since 1966. Tully Lake has many islands to explore and a boat ramp for canoes, kayaks, or boats with a ten-horsepower maximum motor. There are also a picnic area, a shelter with tables which can be reserved, a playground for kids, and a place to play disc golf nearby. The area encompasses many trails. A four-mile Lake Trail encircles the lake and a scenic waterfall located on Lawrence Brook called Doane's Falls.

Doane's Falls and the Tully Lake Campground are both managed by Trustees of Reservations. The tent-only campground on Doane Hill Road has been named in *Yankee Magazine's Special Travel Guide* (2014 May/June issue) as best lake (recreation) in Central Massachusetts. Across from the campground is the Tully River canoe launch where you can put in canoes or kayaks and paddle to Long Pond or enter into Tully Lake. A 7.5 mile mountain bike trail will take you along the Tully River and around Long Pond, as well as a hiking trail. Spirit Falls, also managed by the Trustees of Reservations, cascades down Jacobs Hill and flows into Long Pond.

Some towns have one dam, others none, but Royalston has two. Both dams are managed by Jeff Mangum and are part of a network of flood control dams on tributaries of the Connecticut River. Not only do these dams provide protection from future flooding, but their creation also resulted in recreational opportunities for people to enjoy. The Army Corps of Engineers and Trustees of Reservations have provided the folks of Royalston with an outdoor world of fun right here in our own backyard.

I Knew I Had Found Home

Mara Bright

I've lived forty years in this valley surrounded by gentle hills, home to eagle and coyote, red tail and deer. I stumbled upon the North Quabbin area by accident as a young woman fleeing suburbia in the early 1970s with the intention to find land to homestead on. Twenty-three years of growing food, keeping animals, raising kids, wandering woods and grown-over fields, in a word, nurturing my soul, have bound me to this place. When with my soon-to-be husband and I first saw in Petersham the ramshackle antique cape and land surrounding it, I knew I had found home. In 1973 the highway west beyond Gardner opened into what felt like uncharted territory, unusually wild for a densely populated state, full of protected woods and state forests. And the jewel in the region's crown was the Quabbin Reservoir and watershed.

For years I imagined Quabbin's vastness just over the hills I viewed from my front door. At least twice a week I rambled there, often with the same friend, a woman who loved wandering in the wild as much as I did. We explored hummock and streambed, brambly pasture and forest on the Petersham side of the reservoir, accessing gates from Route 32A and West Road. Sometimes we spent a whole day on our bikes riding from Gate 40 to the baffle dam in Hardwick, partly on pavement, partly on bone-jarring cart roads, discernible only as rutted depressions on the forest floor. We brought a picnic and found a sugar maple to sit under near Dana center or waited to find the perfect expanse of water at the end of a brief bushwhack through the woods. What always seemed best was to find a beach somewhere and a stone to lean against. Pulling out the food we'd brought to share, we sat staring out at the water.

There were other years when we carried kids on our backs or pushed strollers along the pockmarked paved roads. Later we cajoled our kids to walk all the way to the water still a hike for them nonetheless even if we went to Gate 41 or Gate 35—what we called the pie-lady gate because a woman sold homemade pies at a nearby house. We rewarded them with carrot sticks or a handful of crackers and bites of cheese when they got to the top of the next hill or to the lightning-struck oak around the next bend. At the big lake we hefted backpacks from our shoulders to the ground and sat down in warm sand while our kids made piles of pine cones and sticks.

Once in early spring, when water was rushing everywhere and we'd walked all the way downhill with our kids in strollers and backpacks, each of us pushing one child and carrying another, we reached the lake and were greeted by an overcoated exhibitionist. We bundled our kids back up, made up a story to tell them about why we weren't staying, and pressed urgently up the hill again. Another time a neighbor and I stood by as Hector, my black lab, so keenly involved in the chase, followed a beaver into a culvert that connected Pottapaug Pond with a backwater on the other side of the road. Without hesitating, my neighbor kicked off her sneakers and splashed into the culvert after him, pulling him out. At that time I never ventured to the Quabbin alone but still managed to find a friend to go there with me every week so I could receive the nourishment I craved just from standing near the big water. The rest of my week was filled with teaching in schools far from Petersham, caring for children and animals at home, and without fail finding my way into the woods right outside my own dooryard morning and evening.

After leaving Petersham, I lived in the center of New Salem for two years, an invitation to explore another side of the Quabbin. From my apartment I could easily walk to the lookout, a daily destination. From there I catalogued the slow march of seasonal changes reflected underfoot and in the trees I stood beside as I scanned the shoreline below me. Some days I couldn't distinguish between the painted backdrop, suitable for a stage, I seemed to be looking at and the presence of actual islands outlined in tawny sand, red and white pine forests, and everywhere the giant lake. I tried to paint each day's changes on the canvas of my mind. I was there when ragged mist made tree trunks black and glistening and shrouded the scene below me, and on sharp, windy mornings when pine boughs tossed and branches snapped, and the sky and lake were the same vivid blue. In winter I witnessed the water locked in ice, and on the days I stood with snow swirling around me, I strained to see the lake at all when islands, sky, and frozen surface were reduced to shades of white.

By now used to solo adventures, I wandered the shoreline between Millington Road and the end of South Main Street collecting rocks and feathers, an occasional skull, or turtle shell. Once I stumbled upon an enormous tortoise, lumbering through the sand, as ancient as the time of the flooding of the towns that gave themselves to become the

Quabbin, a gift of wildness few could have anticipated. Another time I trained my binoculars on a large, bobbing form that revealed itself to be a deer swimming from the shore to an island. On another morning I sat a few feet away from an otter frolicking and later sunning on a rock and lunching on a fish. On other outings I followed the flight of eagles and turkey vultures. In the fall I checked places where I'd discovered wild grapes and picked enough for jelly. Later I visited spots where I'd noticed cranberries and gathered enough for Thanksgiving relish.

Often I set out for the water with the intention of sitting on the shore with my notebook, recording what was in front of me and waiting for loons to appear. They seldom failed to disappoint me, surprising me with their crazy calls. With binoculars I could see babies ferried on their parents' backs and track loon families paddling with their young, an endless fascination. I rarely saw another human being on these wanderings, and I found refreshment in that solitude.

Who would I be without the beneficence of this place, which throughout my adulthood has been a sanctuary?

photo by Sharon Harmon

Wade Harmon kayaks on Long Pond, Royalston.

Kayaking on Long Pond

Sharon Harmon

Oars dip and glide and
then we slide through blue
glass water, each stroke
mesmerizing and transporting
us to a world of
blue herons, box turtles, water lilies
owls, mountains and refuge.
A tinge of wild grapes in the air
and in the distance the smell of
burning leaves catch the wind
the cut of oars slash the
surface and we float
silently leaving the
everyday world into
postcard scenes
and a world of our best imagining . . .

courtesy of Autumn Light Press, **Swimming with Cats, 2008**

A Town Election in Mid-State

Hugh Field

Having immigrated from eastern Massachusetts, I wrote this account of my first local election experience in May 2006, when we were new to New Salem. Actually things go quite differently. Small town elections in the North Quabbin are low key affairs—a mixture of official ritual and down home Yankee ingenuity.

Two days before our town election, the phone rang. My wife Sharon was asked if she could help with the election. She agreed to staff one of the tables.

On Election Day, we went to the town hall at 11:30 am; the polls did not open until noon. New to town, we opened a basement door on the side of the building and unexpectedly found ourselves in a kitchen. We continued on into the area where the voting would take place, and came upon a crisis—the town safe would not open! Inside the safe was the ballot box for receiving and counting all votes.

The five workers present all rushed around. Ballots were in a pile on a table. My name was on them, as I was a candidate for assessor. But unlike any ballot I had ever seen before, it was printed on two pages stapled together, probably using Microsoft Word or the like.

Soon there was a second commotion: the ballots were wrong. They did not have the correct phrase printed on the outside. Someone went off to print new ballots. The polls would open in about five minutes. How many residents were going to show up? There are about six hundred voters in town. Based on what I had read about past turnouts, I guessed perhaps sixty.

Finally, somebody got the safe open and the ballot box out. Voting booths, four of them, were meanwhile set up at one side of the room. But then, another panic—there were no dividers between the booths, so any voter could look down the line and see how everyone else was voting. Someone went to work on that, and eventually found dividers somewhere.

A minute later, the election officials let me vote as well as the few locals coming in the door. Each first said name and address to an older man at a desk and received a ballot from a tiny elderly woman about four and a half feet tall. Then they proceeded to a voting booth with a curtain where each marked a ballot. After the voters emerged, they stated their names and addresses again to Sharon and put their ballots in the ballot box. "Name side up," said the woman in charge of that as she referred to the front of the document with the word "Ballot." Then voters chatted quietly with the election warden and town clerk. I had remarked to them earlier that my slogan as candidate for assessor could have been "He's fair. He doesn't remember anyone."

Soon I was told apologetically that a candidate could not stand in the soon-to-be voting area, so I went upstairs and looked at an old notice on the bulletin board for a nearby Y2K conference in 1998 that hadn't been taken down. It hung there among other similar postings, many outdated. The building itself looked quite historic, but it was actually built by local people in 1938 to replace the previous town hall building. WPA money funded it together with funds from the community center in the New Salem village of Millington, about to be flooded by the new Quabbin Reservoir.

I left the town hall to go home. Nobody was outside except two large turkeys ambling up. I drove down South Main Street back to Daniel Shays Highway and passed a woman handing out fliers as a write-in candidate for town clerk. The flyer simply said: "so-and-so for town clerk". Next to her on a tree was a sign for town clerk—for someone else. There were no other political signs anywhere in town. I passed West Main Street and continued briefly on North Main Street and onto Daniel Shays Highway, Route 202. I wondered how the town could have had *two* Main Streets—north and south *plus* east and west!

Around five o'clock I returned to the town hall after stopping by the general store for a big bottle of iced tea for the election workers. I brought it to the voting room. The staff had just had sandwiches as an early supper, but there were no voters. Ninety people had voted, though. There was one Question on the ballot: Should the town sign on to the Community Preservation Act? The CPA allows town funds to be used for preservation, the environment, and, incongruously, low-income housing. That might bring in more voters. Sharon was doing fine, but the town had run out of ballots, so they had to print up some more. Good thing they had not been pre-printed!

I went home again and passed the same woman patiently handing out flyers for herself. At seven o'clock, I returned to the town hall for a meeting of the assessors upstairs. To fill a vacancy, I had been appointed a couple of months before, and now the Town had to elect me. A resident wanted a copy of her lot map, so I went up another flight to the only copy machine in the building. It doesn't work properly, and the town couldn't afford to buy another one. In the midst of my trying to make it work, I heard more commotion coming from the basement.

I went back to the assessors' office. Someone said I would certainly win, since I was the only name on the ballot for that position but in future years I would get fewer votes each time, as people got to know me. Assessors, of course, are the people who tell everyone how much their property is valued at, and that determines the property tax each must pay. One of the other assessors announced a month before that he was quitting, and nobody in town was eager to replace him. In fact the previous week, a woman came in to apply for an abatement, and Ken, the assessors' assistant who runs the place, asked her to join the board. She said she might, so Ken hoped to have her appointed.

As nine o'clock rolled around, I wanted the assessors' meeting to end so I could take Sharon home. I went to the voting area, but an hour after the polls closed, vote-counting was not done. I remembered when I had the same job in Shirley thirty miles away and noticed that it takes about as long in person-minutes to count a ballot as to vote. It turned out that exactly two hundred people had voted. If each of the two hundred took a minute to vote and there were later two pairs counting votes, it would take a hundred minutes or an hour and forty minutes for the four people to count the ballots. But it took longer.

One can see why computerized vote-counting has such official appeal, but it can be easily corrupted. Possibly we already got the wrong result for United States president in 2004. Anyway, I kept hearing "Hugh Field, For", from one side, which sounded encouraging. Sharon's twosome sounded quite different, and after a while the officials announced they would have to recount.

I thought of going out for a snack but then realized that the general store, the only store in town, was probably closed, so I found an old book on a shelf to read. After the first pair of counters finished the recount, one approached me. She was quite pleasant and chatty. Finally at 10:30 Sharon's count had balanced. We got up and said goodbye.

Two days later I visited the town clerk in her office opposite the assessors. She had lost as a write-in candidate for re-election because everyone in town knew she would leave soon to join her husband, the ex-assessor, in Texas. Someone said townsfolk had found another write-in candidate, who won—it was the woman with a sign on the tree, not the indefatigable flyer distributor. The defeated town clerk had only had the position since November, and there had been three others just before her. The winner of the 2006 election, however, has held on to the office through the 2014 election. Meanwhile, the community preservation question had been narrowly defeated. Someone said it was because the proponent of the question had recently had the flu.

At the assessors' office, Ken said he would ask the selectboard (towns in this region have backed off the sexist term selectmen) to appoint the woman we met last week. Apparently one must get more than one vote to be elected by write-in, and the only person who got two votes declined the position, so it had to be an appointment.

And I won, as I saw later on the front page of the *Athol Daily News* and in the Greenfield *Recorder*. But I still don't know how many votes I got.

*Like many an avid quilter, Lynn Dudley maintains a healthy stash
of fabric and pre-cut squares.*

The Quilt of Praise

Lynn Dudley

At a doll show coordinated by Elizabeth (Zib) Peirce at Central Congregational Church in Orange in 1991, a few of us admired not only the dolls but also the quilt on which they were arranged. We soon realized we had a shared love of quilting and decided to put on a quilt show the following year. Our newly-formed quilt group consisted of Zib, Winnifred (Winnie) Frye, Irene Hall, and me, all active church members.

After the quilt show in October 1992, we tossed around the idea of making a quilt to celebrate the one-hundredth anniversary of our church building. We agreed that each of us would come up with an idea or two for the quilt and meet again after the holidays.

We got back together in February 1993 and presented our ideas. One was to make squares depicting church life and ecumenical events, then sew them together to make a hanging quilt. Another suggested choosing a traditional quilt pattern like Ocean Wave or Log Cabin or Star of Bethlehem.

All of us had noticed at different times a blank wall to the right of the altar and thought it would be nice to hang something there. The wall was added many years earlier to separate the sanctuary from the then-new Fellowship Hall. It had two large arches to mirror the shape of two stained glass windows on the outside wall to the left of the altar.

So we came up with the idea of a stained-glass-design quilt with a hundred squares showing our church life and events. We gathered ideas for squares from church catalogs, research into the church's history, suggestions and comments from parishioners, and hymn and Bible passages.

We decided to ask people in the congregation to participate by making one or more squares. We offered to help with ideas and supply fabric, but we invited everyone to be creative with ideas, style, and use of materials.

Barbara Kenney, a church member and accomplished crewel stitcher, agreed to embroider the three top panels which I drew—a peace dove with an olive branch beneath a radiating star in the center, the nativity scene to the left, and an empty cross and rainbow to the right.

Joseph Bergeron installs brackets to hang the Central Congregational Church quilt.

In place of stained glass, quilted sections make up the sensational nine-by-fourteen-foot quilt designed by Lynn Dudley and made by congregants of Central Congregational Church, Orange, in the 1990s for a windowless church niche.

Below the top panels would be six smaller squares, two to be quilted interpretations of paintings by congregant and local artist Ralph Henley. One would show how the church looked when rebuilt on its present site in 1893 after the fire of 1891. The other would show the church as it looks today.

Beneath them would be ninety even smaller squares. Themes covered a multitude of special church memories and events, both past and present, and general church motifs. Among many outstanding squares was one depicting the church in its original state prior to an 1891 fire and another showing the devastation after the hurricane of 1938. A beautiful poem by beloved parishioner Mary Coit, embroidered by Zib, poignantly reminded everyone of her. A list of our ministers over the past hundred years, Bible passages, hymns, and other creative expressions of love completed the ninety squares.

All told, there were thirty-eight square makers including one man and three young people.

With the stained-glass motif as the outer border and counting the whole quilt itself as a square, we had one hundred squares to represent one hundred years.

Zib donated fabric for sashing between the large and medium panels and small-squares panels. "I've had this cloth for a long time," Zib said, "but never could find a use for it till now." The rest of us raided our stashes and chipped in to purchase fabric for the stained-glass borders, backing, and batting.

Our excitement grew each week as quilters completed more squares and turned them in to us. Congregants constantly asked us, "How's it coming along? When do you think it'll be done? Do you need me to make any more squares?" Enthusiasm throughout the church thrilled everyone.

For many Tuesdays, Thursdays, and Saturday mornings through that year, we laughed together and arranged, rearranged, and stitched squares and sashing and panels until it was all put together. Then came the task of quilting the top to the batting and backing. We completed it in March, 1994.

Alan Prouty donated framing material. My husband Joe Bergeron built the frame for the fourteen-by-nine-foot quilt and hung it in the sanctuary with much laughter and supervision from the quilt group.

We presented it to the congregation on Easter morning, April 3, 1994, to a warm and enthusiastic standing ovation. We all agreed it was a labor of love. It decorates the church to this day more than twenty years later.

photo courtesy of Lynn Dudley

Lynn and committee plotted the quilt on graph paper with accompanying notes. Church members created squares.

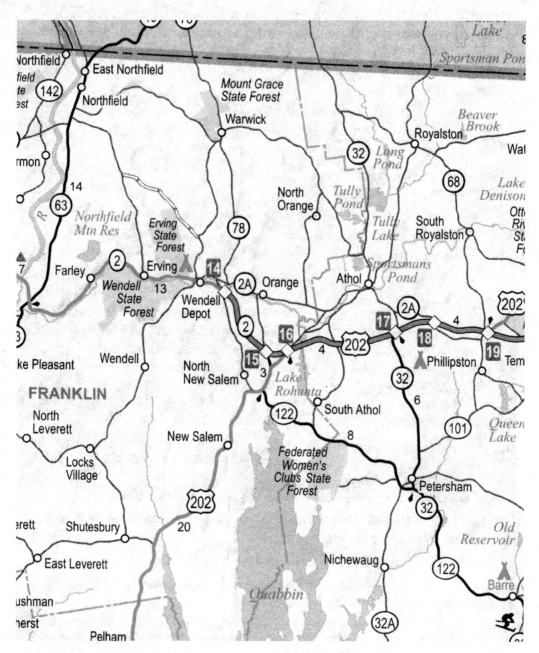

Although he lives in San Francisco, Jon Chaisson misses the North Quabbin where he grew up. Fortunately, he says, Half Moon Bay, California, thirty miles from his home, looks a bit like the North Quabbin. When Jon visits the North Quabbin, he loves to drive around. Here's a printed map of major roads in North Quabbin and environs for drivers without a GPS.

On the Road Redux or I Left My Heart in Central Massachusetts

Jon Chaisson

One of my favorite things to do in the North Quabbin area is road-tripping. There may be an ultimate destination in mind, maybe just outside the area, but part of the enjoyment is getting there. On weekends I jump in the car, stop at a local mom-and-pop in uptown Athol for a large coffee to go (the New Englander's regular, of course, cream and two sugars), and be on my way. I throw some music on, often one of my own mixtapes, and let my mind wander as I enjoy the views. It's a release from the week's work stresses and a Zen-like enjoyment of nature as it happens.

Driving north up Route 32, I pass the vast stretch of Silver Lake Cemetery where I spent hot summers working for the town so many years ago. I cross over Tully Dam, its rocky façade giving the impression that the road is held up by nothing but a pile of boulders with a lovely view of the lake below. My dad took a picture of us in his old station wagon at the picnic area down there . . . I must have been four or five at the time, but I remember that moment well, my sisters and I all peeking out of the back passenger window with wide, toothy smiles. Once I motor past the dam, it's like I am in another world, a forested world of pines and wild birds and cabin-sized houses, wisps of smoke coming from woodstove flues. I forget the rest of the world is out there for a while, bound as I am by the forest, and it calms me.

Sometimes I head over the state border and up to Keene, or I turn left at Richmond and head down to Winchester. Other times I take one of the side roads and head towards North Orange instead. That's one of my favorite routes. I take the circuit up there and head back via Route 78, cutting through Warwick past Mount Grace and past the quaint triangular town common, sometimes continuing down 78 to its terminus, sometimes turning at Athol Road and sneaking back through Tully. There are numerous back roads up there that will bring you back home, and they're all hiding stories--family houses, pondside cabins, people's lives. I never think about asking these people what they're doing living out in the middle of nowhere or asking them what drew them out there in the first place, finding their inspiration. It's home. It's where one is supposed to be.

photo by Marcia Gagliardi

Taking a wintry back road from Route 202 in New Salem rewards, sometimes, with an unencumbered view of a sunset.

Sometimes I head down South Athol Road, aware of that curious land grading a short way into the woods, all that remains of the old Athol and Enfield Railroad line from nearly a century ago. Possibly I take that shortcut on Partridgeville Road that would take me to Route 202 and points further south, if I so desired. I stay on this road, thinking about its history so far ago as the former Route 21. Most of that highway is under water now, taken over by the Quabbin Reservoir. If I keep going on South Athol Road, I'll eventually merge briefly with Route 122 and then onto Old North Dana Road. I keep going and hit one of the Quabbin gates. I continue on foot, past a couple of old house foundations, and eventually I get to water. The Reservoir stretches southward for miles, for a third of the state, out of my view-nothing but birds, wild animals, the occasional fisherman, and nature.

When I drive up Bearsden Road to Adams Farm slaughterhouse and buy local produce in the retail store, I enjoy the view from the parking lot noting how peaceful downtown Athol looks from there, so unassuming in that valley below, and how stunningly gorgeous the hills are in high foliage season. We're a small community that doesn't always get talked about, but we've got beauty in spades when it comes to the autumnal change in colors. I stop driving, ----get out of the car and walk for a while here, listen to the land, watch its circles of life.

The road down Daniel Shays Highway towards Amherst is burned into my memory, since I traveled it countless times towards the Five College area, stopping at the general store in the center of New Salem, picking up a snack or two, saying hi to whoever's at the register. It's a nice day, so it's worth stopping for a soda. Rolling down the window, heading further south, I enter Shutesbury for about a thousand feet and re-enter New Salem seconds later and hold my breath the entire time—just to say I did.

Points east and west are more heavily traveled roads, Route 2, the state's northern east-west highway. I know these roads well through my many and varied commutes to various jobs. I made it a point to know as many ways to work without getting on a single major highway, and while it didn't exactly save on time, it made for a much quieter and more enjoyable trip. But taking Route 2 west of Orange is an enjoyable trip as well, driving tandem with the Millers River, passing by the occasional roadside fisherman, catching a deer taking a quick drink on the opposite shore before slipping back into the forest.

Half Moon Bay, California, shown above, and its environs remind Jon Chaisson of the North Quabbin.

I'm still not quite used to the new stretch of road high above the paper mill, remembering countless times back in the day when I'd have to stop for a trailer backing into a delivery bay or for its workers crossing the road during shift change. Coming into the quaint center of Erving, I remember the days we'd turn off there and head up to Laurel Lake for a bit of summer swimming and the old scarecrow family in the Farley section of town. Driving east, I head to the old town fairs on Phillipston and Templeton commons, taking back roads to Gardner, taking the roller-coaster road up to the Red Apple Farm or further up to South Royalston, a sort-of short cut to Winchendon. Never a shortage of places to go.

I live on the opposite coast now in the quiet Richmond District neighborhood in the northwestern corner of San Francisco. If I crane my neck right now, I can see autumn orange-red twin towers of the Golden Gate Bridge and the rolling Marin Headlands across the way. I couldn't get any further west from my hometown if I tried. It's a great place to live. And yet . . .

And yet, wherever I go here in the Bay Area, I'm constantly reminded of my hometown area. Walking through the wooded terrain of the Presidio reminds me of walking through the woods surrounding my parents' house south of downtown Athol. Meandering through Golden Gate Park I can watch bison graze, herons sifting through swampy inlets, model boats buzzing around on a small lake just like the many farms and lakes I'd pass back home. The lovely winding back roads of Sonoma and Napa Valley are very much like driving through rural farming areas of Phillipston and Royalston complete with roadside produce stands and wide stretches of rolling farmland. The small town of Half Moon Bay is similar to Athol with its main strip of small stores, family restaurants, and close-knit community. There are so many places out here in the Bay Area that bring memories of being back east. And when I head there to visit family, I get to relive those memories again.

I may have left the North Quabbin area nearly a decade ago, but it's never left me. Not really.

Reverend Cynthia Crosson-Harrington often travels with her service dog, the Shih Tzu Dandi.

Gone to the Dogs?

Cynthia Crosson-Harrington

Those who are proud to be residents of the North Quabbin area might bridle a bit if they were told the region is going to the dogs, but this can actually be a positive thing. The dogs I mention are of the highest order—trained service dogs for ministry.

How does one train a dog for the ministry, one might ask, envisioning perhaps a "seminary for canines." The dogs in question were trained at NEADS/Dogs for Deaf and Disabled Americans, a Princeton, Massachusetts based agency dedicated to placing dogs to promote independence for those who are disabled. But as they train for this role, some dogs distinguish themselves not as one-person service dogs but rather as those better suited for work with groups of people. I used to say that my own service dog for ministry "flunked Service Dog 101," but his trainer admonished me to frame my dog's own disability (a fear of loud noises) as something that made him more suited for the ministry. After all, how helpful would it be if a dog helping a disabled person ran under the nearest chair at the sound of a car backfire. But, as his trainer advised, we are a bit more lenient in clerical circles.

My favorite story about why one dog entered the ministry involves a beautiful Golden Retriever trained by NEADS. It was decided well into his training that the dog was not service dog material because with no apparent provocation, he would look off in the distance totally distracted from his task and seemingly attend to something that no one else could see or perhaps hear. Short of this strange habit, he was a wonderful dog. His trainer concluded he was better suited to alternative service. Someone teasingly commented that since he appeared to be hearing voices, the ministry might be the vocation for this dog.

The first service dog for ministry in the North Quabbin area was partnered with Virginia Evans. Ginny and Lynks, a salt-and-pepper Standard Schnauzer, began their ministry together in June of 1998, and he accompanied her to the Community Church of North Orange and Tully where Ginny was a student minister. Ginny would later tell me how integral Lynks was to her ministry as he joined her on pastoral visits and added his own special brand of ministry to hers.

In 2000, I became a student in ministerial field placement at that same small church under the mentorship of Reverend Lois Buchiane. Reverend Lois was a pioneer in her own right and probably thoroughly enjoyed having something as unusual as a dog share her student's time. I first met Ginny and Lynks when we—Lois's several former students and I, the student in residence—traveled to Andover-Newton Theological School to support Lois as she received her award for excellence in supervision. As we all piled into the van taking us to the event, I was surprised when Ginny jumped in with her dog garbed in his NEADS vest designating his service dog status. As we talked about his role in Ginny's ministry, I was captivated. Having been raised not only with dogs but also in the home of my minister Dad, I was fascinated by the role that dogs could play in the ministry.

Soon after that trip, I approached NEADS and learned that a minister must be actively involved with his or her vocation in order to receive a ministry dog. Not surprisingly I was on the doorstep of NEADS the week after I graduated from seminary, since I knew I would be helping out in North Orange until I had my own call to a church.

The dogs of my childhood had been large—mostly German Shepherds that my family raised—and I imagined myself accompanied by a large, regal dog as I walked down the aisle of my church. When the NEADS trainer presented me with the twelve wriggling pounds of grey fluff—a little Shih Tzu—that had been chosen for me, I was a bit surprised, but I was quickly won over. Dandi would become my shadow, my companion, my helpmate, and an invaluable part of my ministry over the next nine years to date.

Having a service dog for ministry brings a whole new dimension to ministry. Dandi is not only an icebreaker for those who might be hesitant to approach or even to confide in me as a minister, but he provides an element of humor that relaxes even the most uptight church goer. One Palm Sunday, I was preaching in the Petersham Congregational Church which looked quite festive with its array of scattered palms. I was well into my sermon when I was distracted by a tentative wave from a woman seated in the front pew. So urgent was her gesturing that I stopped my oratory and asked "Yes?"

"He's eating a palm," she whispered in a loud voice. Sure enough, my canine ministerial assistant was happily munching on a palm. Not knowing if palms are poisonous, I quickly jumped from the pulpit to grab it from his mouth.

Dandi looked up at me resolutely as if to say, "Well, you had gone on too long anyway." It might not be surprising that I never got to finish my sermon, but the congregation will probably never forget that worship service.

From snatching an accidentally dropped piece of communion bread (his first communion) to retrieving a paper fluttering from the pulpit, Dandi keeps me on my toes and the congregation engaged. He is also the only one encouraged to sleep through my sermons. But his special love is children. I often use him in children's stories explaining that D-O-G is the mirror image of G-O-D. Once when I was preaching in Warwick, a child had brought his stuffed animal, which he clutched lovingly. Dandi assumes that all stuffed animals are his toys and was anxious to make it his own. I gave him a command not to touch the toy as I gathered the children in a circle around me for their story.

Dandi sat uneasily beside me, eyes glued on the stuffed bear, body tensed hoping that I would release him to retrieve it. As the story concluded with my customary prayer with the children and it became evident to my canine helper that he would not be allowed to claim the prize, he uttered a long "awwrh"—a quite indescribable noise of utter frustration. A voice from the front pew chuckled, "That was Amen," perhaps not realizing that in that small church, the comment was heard by all and elicited hearty laughter. Dandi gazed up at me with a clear "Is it something I did?"

Lest it seem that the presence of a ministry dog leads to irreverence, I should say that Dandi is most respectful during prayers. He curls up beside me and is the model of the reverent churchgoer. I am thankful that he has as yet not chosen to join in the hymns as he does sometimes when I am choosing them for the bulletin. In preparation for Sunday worship, I use an online website that plays the music for hymns. The website augments my less-than-expert ability to read music, so I can hear the tunes and determine if I want to use a hymn. Dandi has been known to join in when he fancies a particular piece. His melodious howl is sometimes louder than the music!

Ministry dogs also provide a wonderful resource for pastoral care. Dandi, donned in his official red NEADS service dog vest, accompanies me on pastoral visitations in some hospitals and nursing homes. His calm, warm, and engaging presence brings joy to many an ill person. One visit to an Alzheimer's unit brought words to the lips of a man who had not spoken for some time as he imagined that Dandi was his beloved former pet. It also brought tears to the eyes of his loving wife who longed to hear her husband speak again. These would be her husband's last words as he stroked my little Shih Tzu with a peaceful smile on his lips.

Other clergy in the North Quabbin area have recognized the grace that a dog brings to ministry and have applied to and received dogs from NEADS. For a time, Waldo, also a Shih Tzu, accompanied Reverend Jean Thompson of the Community Church of North Orange and Tully. Reverend Michelle LaGrave, formerly pastor of the Petersham Unitarian Church, welcomed Bella, a lovely black Labrador Retriever into her ministry.

I believe that my fellow clergy will attest to the richness of having a canine assistant. It may take a while to accept that your dog will often be greeted before you are: "Hello, Dandi, you cute little thing. Oh,. Hi, Reverend Cynthia." But it is heartwarming to see the effect these animals have on everyone they meet. How blessed we in the North Quabbin have been to have had four such ministerial assistants.

To Build a Barn

Doris Bittenbender, sometimes thinking aloud in italics (written in conference with Karl Bittenbender)

Well, that's three in favor of Plan C and one in favor of Plan B.

The one would be me.

So, I guess we move on with the project. We (two parents and two grown children) had all agreed that something needed to be done with the barn. It was over 150 years old, was leaning to the east (downhill), and needed major renovation to remain standing. However, we disagreed over what to do with the "post-demolition barn."

Plan A: do nothing

Plan B: build a new barn/garage, much smaller, stick construction, cheaper and faster

Plan C: demolish all but the post and beam frame and rebuild.

Dinner-table conversation over. We are going to rebuild the barn.

The next step was to bring in some barn consultants to advise and give us some estimates. All recommended saving the frame. Most gave us quotes on reconstruction that are way beyond our budget, but one (who admired the frame the most) said he would be happy to work with Karl, advising and helping when needed but allowing Karl to do the bulk of the work. Of course, it might take a long time. *Here we go.* But it also would be more affordable. We committed to at least begin by hearing his recommendations and estimates of what would be involved in salvaging the barn frame and rebuilding from there.

Old New England farmhouses usually had a barn, some attached to the house either directly or by various connecting structures. Obviously, this allowed for the farmer to reach his animals more easily in the intense winters; it also gave the frugal Yankee farmer lots of space to store "stuff that might be needed someday." Our barn was attached in the manner of house to breezeway to garage to barn, and it was especially handy during the cold nights of lambing season. By this stage, though, we had no farm animals, and one might argue that the barn was superfluous, even though it did hold its share of "useful someday" items. Karl's mantra was that "this house had a barn when we moved in, and I want it to have a barn when we leave . . . a barn that will last another 150 years. It will be all finished in three years."

After a family meeting, the Bittenbenders decided to deconstruct and then reconstruct their old barn, above, with an eye toward preserving the original timber frame.

About midway through deconstruction, the original timber frame showed itself a sturdy skeleton for rebuilding.

photos on these pages by Karl Bittenbender

Well, it took five, but who's counting.

We looked at books. We circled the area towns and looked at every barn we drove past, of which there were many in a condition similar to ours. Didn't we sort of "owe" it to history to restore it? We stood in the road and envisioned what it would look like. That was hard when we were looking at a structure in place so we began the demolition. Just to see how it would go.

We could always change our minds and reconsider Plan A or Plan B.

First to go was the garage. This required hiring a crane, but most of the labor was done by Karl, slowly and carefully. Next we demolished the shed attached to the south side of the barn.

This we knew we would not replace. Long six-by-sixes and six-by-eights were saved for re-use. What remained was a large forty-by-fifty-foot structure with five bents, four bays. It was a "bank" barn —built with a street level entrance in the front and a "basement" below with open access to the field downhill. The stone piles used for support under the barn needed to be replaced with a foundation. And a foundation needs to have water control, which means digging surrounding ditches, which means buying a backhoe which would attach to the Kubota tractor, also bought with this project in mind.

Hmmm . . . moving right along.

The backhoe made the ditches possible and also facilitated moving rocks from the fields behind the house to be put in place for construction of a dry stone foundation.

In order to work on the foundation, we needed to lift the barn structure. We accomplished this by attaching lift blocks to all twenty standing posts. After they were in place, the building mover arrived and constructed four corner cribs to support the steel beams that would in turn lift the building. The actual lift was completed in a half day. Most of the walls were removed, but the roof remained in place to give the structure some strength while suspended. It looked like any old barn, just six feet up in the air.

Then it was time to remove the floor and construct the stone foundation. We expected to lower the barn back down on a new foundation and floor within a few months but an injury to Karl's back while tearing out the old floor set us back almost another year.

Meanwhile, the "flying barn" brought many onlookers . . . and some questions as to whether Karl would ever finish this project.

Even though I wasn't enthused at the beginning, by now I had confidence that he would indeed finish. Those who know him know that Karl likes to solve problems. Other people's problems. Town problems. Building problems. And this barn was certainly a problem.

Once he was back on the job, Karl had what was for him probably the most pleasurable part of the project—choosing and placing dry stone for the foundation. Framing and pouring the grade beam with assistance from friends and neighbors followed placing the foundation. He knew that at this point he needed a work crew. Up until then, he had handled the bulk of the work himself. Even though many friends had volunteered to help throughout the span of the project, he inevitably had to turn them down. As he was inclined to say, "I don't know what *I'm* doing, so I can't really tell *you* what to do."

A completed floor of laminated veneer lumber (LVLs) and manufactured floor joists topped by plywood and further topped by the salvaged floor boards brought us to the point where the barn could be lowered back into place. While the barn was suspended, Karl and his helpers repaired and readied posts. There was a lot of creaking and sighing as the posts again took the weight of the barn and temporary steel beams were removed.

Some things you choose not to do when you are over seventy years old.

Ahh . . . wise decision.

So we hired a roofing contractor with a young, agile team to resurface the roof. We decided that soon after its completion we would also hire another contractor to install solar panels. He placed twenty-four panels, enough to provide at least two times our current electric needs.

Now walls. The barn originally had a layer of pine boards covered by siding. The interior layer was in good shape, so Karl installed it again on the inside walls of the barn, all to be covered on the outside by new pine boards in a giant board-and-batten manner. The process took much longer than imagined because Karl was a one-man work force handling sixteen-foot boards, not to say I wasn't helpful when I could be.

As Karl replaced the walls, we decided to leave a large opening in the back of the barn, thinking of times in our past when we had to back

127

a hay wagon into the barn in order to unload. A back opening would give drive-through access to the barn and hayloft. A ramp (more stones to place) brought access out from the barn and down to the field below.

The front of the barn then had the original large opening in need of doors. These Karl constructed from sixteen-foot one-bys of varied widths. Once swung into place with a complex pulley assembly, they opened and closed easily on a set of trollies. As Karl fashioned the doors, I enjoyed time by his side, assisting when I could. Looking from the barn through the open door to the east, the view is of a hay field sloping gradually downward. It drops and crosses Tully Brook, but from this vantage point, your eyes don't see the brook and you look across to Chestnut Hill in Athol. It's a bucolic country scene. Viewed from the center of the barn, it has the appearance of a picture, the door and barn walls framing the scene. Your eyes see only that portion of the scene, and since there are no surrounding views to draw your eyes from the center, the view becomes more focused and vibrant. Turning your head around and looking through the open door to the west you see another picture, similarly framed and drawing you into the driveway, road, and woods beyond. Roadside trees appear larger and more defined.

Interesting.

So many people, friends and strangers alike, stopped to follow our progress. A neighbor who frequently walked by commented "I haven't seen that barn straight in seventy years." As we drive through our town and neighboring towns, we see many barns, probably of a similar vintage as ours, falling down or nearly doing so. There is an expense in salvaging them, not an easy one to meet. We were fortunate in that Karl was able to do the bulk of the work himself.

Me, yeah, I'm happy with Plan C. It looks like it is right where it belongs.

The rebuilt Bittenbender barn sports solar panels.

Chainsaw carver Sue O'Sullivan of Royalston gave lots of life to her woody companion, a twelve-foot representation of a grizzly bear.

Making Art with a Chainsaw

Sharon Harmon

There are chainsaw carvers and there are chainsaw carvers, but as a chainsaw carver, spunky Sue O'Sullivan is a bird of a different feather. Eight years ago, Sue O'Sullivan, who moved to Royalston from England in 1986, decided to try her hand at chainsawing trees into representations of indigenous animals. She had first learned how to use a chainsaw when she needed to cut wood to supply heat for her home.

When you see Sue, who is fairly small and trim with long dark hair and twinkling blue eyes, she is the last person you would envision as wielding a chainsaw to make a twelve-foot grizzly bear or a lion, owl, eagle, angel, or even a large flower planter. She considers herself a Renaissance woman as she is largely self-taught. She has been doing art in the form of pen and inks, acrylics, and pyrography (a technique used to burn pictures onto mushrooms). Sue is FBI-certified for composite drawings and does pet photos and buildings to round out her repertoire.

In front of Sue's farm style home, there are two huge carved bears. One has a mailbox in its stomach. The bears are on display with other pieces on the property. Sue's smallest carving at eighteen inches is of two black Labs.

"Soft white pine is the easiest to work with," she said. "Wood needn't be a certain age, and it can still be in the ground. Trees often have pine borers in them, and the borers eventually make holes through the middle. First I peel bark off trees, and there are lots of grubs inside that spatter all over me when the chainsaw gets to them. It's pretty gross, but it's part of the job."

Sometimes Sue draws her ideas on paper, but usually working from her natural artist's instincts, she just starts to carve.

Sue's fiancé loves what she does. "He is learning how to carve," she said and pointed out a cute little bear he had done. Sue attends a yearly event in Ridgeway, Pennsylvania called The Ridgeway Chainsaw Rendezvous. "Approximately two hundred carvers participate for a week and do their art," she remarked. "Then they auction off their pieces for fund raisers." She is one of few women involved in the event.

"I use scaffolding for large pieces, although I'm not crazy about heights. I'm trying to overcome my fear of them," she added. One of Sue's favorite projects was working on a tree in Orange, with Mike Legassey and Mark Bosworth, two other carvers for The North Quabbin Tree Project. It was also one of the scariest because of the heights, but Sue was able to pull it off. The tree is located at 145 South Main Street and is indeed a lot of fun to see. The workmanship of the three carvers is apparent, as there are countless animals, birds, and reptiles to view. The most meaningful carving to Sue was an angel she did to relieve stress from a former job she had as a dispatcher. It was in memory of a three-year-old child who died.

Sue works on commission and is a veritable powerhouse of energy. She can be seen on Facebook and can also be reached at renaissancegirlartwork.com.

Surrounded by gear, Sue O'Sullivan works on a chainsaw carving.

photo by David Brothers

Passersby in the North Quabbin sometimes happen upon a chainsaw carving of an animal or whimsical character by chainsaw artists including Sue O'Sullivan, Mike Legassey, and Mark Bosworth.

A menagerie populates a tree at 145 South Main Street, Orange, carved by Sue O'Sullivan, Mike Legassey, and Mark Bosworth. A buck peeks out, above.

photo on these pages by David Brothers

Among the creatures taking up real estate on the South Main Street, Orange, tree is a great blue heron.

Jonathan and Susan von Ranson collaborate, above, on their non-electric Wendell home, which they built themselves with town variances and in the spirit of North Quabbin (and especially Wendell) back-to-the-landers.

Polygamy and the Woods at Night in Wendell

Jonathan von Ranson

A boss I had back in the sixties, a non-regulation guy, charismatic, attracted to men, who lived with his wife and showered in his back yard within view of his neighbors, once mentored me to "be a bit more polygamous, Jonathan. It's smothering to be too monogamous."

The idea, even though I thought it might be self-serving on my boss's part, fanned something slow-burning in me. I'd learned even before marriage that to be sexually poly, as massively attractive as it was in theory, was just too stressful on my emotional constitution with its 1942 German-New England instruction manual. But there are ramifications, equally taboo, that I have been to bed with—a broader kind of polygamy that he might have actually had in mind, unorthodox love adventures as dangerous to complacency as trysts, release, obsession, companionship, regret, and other potential sources of vitality and growth.

The beating pulse of the idea, in fact, may have drawn me to Wendell. It became an almost sexual desire to have some real land with trees and water that weren't planted or arranged. And in retrospect, wasn't it essentially the urge to expand out of too-tidy containers: nuclear family, business organization, quarter-acre suburban plot, civilization? To desire some *real land* smacks of the call of that dark-haired stranger, Nature. It's a polygamous urge.

In March, 1972 I bought sixty deeply landlocked acres hemmed in by Wendell State Forest on one side and steep mountainside on the other. I slipped off whenever I could to visit this place of—to me—escape, physicality, personality, comfort, and surprise. I brought my first wife and our kids many times to camp on it, too, trying to act innocent. But the land and I had our secrets!

Like the time I arrived once, alone, at dusk. I bushwhacked my way in search of a lookout I'd spotted on an earlier visit. Sitting on a small rock, I ate a sandwich out of a bag as the sky darkened, then unrolled my bedding on some moss.

Nictophobia—fear of the dark, of the woods at night—had plagued me all my life. That night in a green Sears sleeping bag, I did hand-to-hand combat with sinister, flesh-hungry half-beings. I heard mutterings. Rustlings and twig breakage . . . footsteps? Crashing sounds, almost. *OK, I said, get a grip. What headlines have you seen — Black Bear Mauls Massachusetts Man as He Sleeps Outside? Camper Murdered by Night-Stalking Hillbilly with Mouthful of Rotten Teeth . . . ?*

Sleep finally came. Fear subsided. The Big Dipper did a quarter circuit around the North Star, making a staccato advance each time I briefly came to. When I finally awoke to a breathless, blue-sky morning, I'd put nictophobia behind me. I didn't know it, nor that, many a dark night, I would be walking two miles through the woods to my home on this land.

It was six years later—1978—that my kids and I finally discovered the human community the area supported. Characters--people with welcome in their pupils and easy hugs. They'd stepped off the path, too, and found a place that reflected wild spirit and seemed to warm, challenge, and nurture it. At first, the long-timers had held the new ones at arm's length. Soon, though, the cultural center of gravity shifted and the town became peculiarly encouraging of a rare human unfolding.

So much so that, in the mid-eighties, a woman, red-faced and sputtering at a meeting in Erving about the Route 2 relocation fight, pointed to our Bear Mountain. "They *ought* to put that highway through," she exploded. "Open that place up, up there . . . find out what's going on!"

Today, it seems like it would take a small nuke and a couple dozen gas wells to re-fold the wings of community spirit here. We've spent our night in the wilderness, known the bleakness of living in fear. Communal love does a steady surge as the reference point, organizing principle, a common political metabolism moving us forward. With rare togetherness and little ego, we're working our way toward neglected rudiments of life: threatened essences and compacts, existential matters, great questions of life, culture, and purpose. Doing so by way of long-term commitments like the Full Moon Coffee House and ongoing big-topic library groups or shorter ones like keeping Wendell's lizards, frogs, turtles, and post office from becoming road kill, or authorizing—meticulously but nonetheless subversively—a non-electric dwelling in the center of town (involving my now-wife, Susan, and me).

In spirit, what's happening in Wendell is reminiscent of the intelligence, freedom, and courage of the unconquered wild, the embracing, polygamous condition: love of other, of place, and ever day more passionately, of the live-giving whole. It's that threatening, untidy, and hopeful.

Wendell's not a total anomaly. Other towns in the area hover close to the paradigm's edge as well. But our broad little ridgetop somewhere between the Connecticut River and Mount Wachusett, the Quabbin and the Millers River might have enjoyed a particular historic head start. Civilized European thinking never fully overtook this place; the order to fear the dark and wild and embrace the man-made and think homogeneously was never officially implemented here. Credit the swampy, difficult-to-exploit soils and terrain, the thousands of acres of state forest, Audubon and MDC land. The way we're suspended in terms of urban gravity in a lonely place in space, as evidence the old loggers and farmers who sometimes would walk eight miles to a small town or fifteen miles to a bigger one . . . forty-five to Springfield.

The hippie influx threw off the Realtors. Along with hardscrabble old farmhouses, defunct sawmills and the occasional mobile home, visitors in the eighties could make out through the trees humble, owner-built houses bearing a make-do look. It suggested rebellious, possibly poetic inclinations on the part of the population and the definite waft of marijuana. A town character sufficiently wild to allow it, with some organized efforts as well, to dodge the bullet of commodity housing.

The risky, collective dedication to innerness, outerness, togetherness . . . wilderness . . . whole life bespoke, and still bespeaks, Wendell's essential polygamy, a more fully human practice of love.

When Don and Janee Stone bought their house and land in Wendell, they knew it included the crypt built in the early 1800s for Moses and Patty Stone, not related to Don and Janee. A practiced storyteller, Don wove a special story about the crypt for his and Janee's children, Greg, Steve, and Serena.

Birth of a Legend

Don Stone

I have always loved stories.

When I was a boy, almost every night my dad would tell stories to my two brothers and me. We were always the heroes, and the entire solar system was our playground. We had grand devices made of exotic materials like impervium, which could bore through the center of the earth. We could fly through the sun and even travel backward and forward through time.

When I became a dad, I continued the tradition. Every night was story time. Sometimes we would read—great tales like *The Hobbit, Watership Down,* and *The Lord of the Rings.* But making up my own stories was more satisfying—and more fun. I usually began my stories in "ordinary reality," then see how far imagination could carry without violating certain unwritten rules. For example, you could not get out of a tough predicament the story had wound for its heroes (now my kids) by having them wake up and discover it was only a dream. But you had to get them back home. The stories always ended up coming back home.

We moved to Wendell in 1970. Gregg was eight, Steve six, and Serena just two. It was an exciting move for all of us, from a modern house in Hanover, New Hampshire with a small yard and lots of neighbors to a rambling, two-hundred-year-old Cape Cod farmhouse on a dirt road surrounded by woods, way out in the country. Exploring our new home was a grand adventure of discovery and a fertile source of ideas for new stories.

Shortly after moving in, we had a chance meeting with Eleanor Goddard, wife of Wendell's chief of police and a lifelong resident of Wendell. She said she was born and grew up just a half mile down Jennison Road from our house in a Cape-style cottage similar to ours but now abandoned and decaying. Surely this seventy-year-old woman with impish eyes and an infectious smile would know some of the history of our new home. We asked and she did but went on to say, "First let me go talk with Susie Bean. She knows everything."

Eleanor promised to stop by the next week with more information. And she did, exclaiming that Susie Bean had a lot to say about the history of our house.

The story she told us was remarkable. Our house was built in the late 1790s by Moses Stone, who was the local stonemason. And he was very skilled at his craft. Our house sits on a foundation of carefully cut and shaped rectangular granite blocks, each about six feet long by eighteen inches high and eight inches thick. Our house, with the original hand-hewn sills, floor joists, and floor boards, remains level and plumb two hundred years later. We also found Moses's quarry, a long, exposed granite ledge that still clearly shows evidence of hand drilling and splitting off of slabs. Many rejected slabs still litter the site, now reclaimed by Wendell forest.

Moses, with his wife Patty, lived in and farmed the homestead until the 1850s. Eleanor went into great detail relating a story about the building of the crypt that still sits on our land by the pond, about two hundred yards from the house. Patty would sit in the field under a parasol giving emotional support to her husband as he constructed the crypt out of massive and skillfully shaped slabs of granite. Each slab was so carefully worked that they fit together perfectly, forming an underground vault about five feet by eight feet with a six-foot-high ceiling formed by three granite slabs. It took Moses all summer to complete the structure, with Patty watching and providing encouragement and cool drinks. Susie Bean said that Moses and Patty loved their land so much they wanted to remain there forever. When they died, Moses and Patty were both interred in the crypt until the property passed out of family ownership and the bodies were moved to the cemetery in the center of Wendell.

In the months that followed Susie Bean's story told to us by Eleanor Goddard, we were able to corroborate names and dates with records at the Franklin County Registry of Deeds. We found Moses and Patty's headstones in the Wendell cemetery. We have never been able find a genealogical connection between us and our home's original builders and owners, but we share the same name and certainly feel connected.

We did find out more about Susie Bean, though. She was Eleanor Goddard's mother, who had died in 1940.

So a two-hundred-year-old house with a history, a large barn with hand-hewn beams, sitting on granite pillars, and even a mysterious crypt built into the bank overlooking the pond provide abundant material for exploration, imagination, and storytelling.

The first time my kids and I went over to explore the crypt, not sure what might be inside, we were greeted by a huge black snake, as thick as my wrist. We found no bodies when we pried open the vine-locked door, but we did find a dark stone vault full of ghosts and echoes of stories past.

Another enigmatic feature of our house we quickly discovered was a beehive structure formed by the three fireplaces built around the central chimney. This is a common feature in authentic Cape-style construction from that period. Entry to the beehive is gained through a secret door in the back of the only closet in the house. Large enough for several adults to stand, it is a perfect hiding place. We wondered how it might have been used in the two-hundred-year history of our house, definitely a story waiting to be told.

And so one of my first stories took Gregg, Steve, and Serena back in time to the 1850s, living on the small farm in Wendell which was now our home. In the story, the farm was part of the Underground Railroad. One summer night, neighbors from New Salem arrived at the Stone house in a horse-drawn wagon with a load of hay. Hidden in the hay was a family fleeing northward, escaping from slavery. They were pursued by evil bounty hunters from the South.

Gregg, Steve, and Serena helped to sneak the family into their house and gave them some food and water. The runaways included a mom and dad and two children, a brother and sister the same ages as Gregg and Steve. They told amazing stories of their escape from a plantation in North Carolina and their long and difficult journey north toward freedom. Especially frightening were the several narrow escapes from the evil bounty hunters and their vicious dogs.

This was very serious business. Gregg, Steve, and Serena knew all about the Underground Railroad and their parents' secret membership in it. They knew that the secret room in the center of the house would be the hiding place if bounty hunters came near. They also knew about the tunnel that had been dug from the beehive out to the crypt, providing an emergency escape, should the beehive be discovered.

But this was the first time an escaping family had actually come to their house. It was thrilling and fun to be with new-found friends. But when they heard, later that night, that bounty hunters with their dogs were seen in New Salem, it became really scary. Gregg and Steve led the escaping family into the secret room just before the bounty hunters with their snarling dogs invaded the house. It was time to use the secret passage.

Finding no runaways in the house, the bounty hunters searched the barn and other outbuildings. When they came to the crypt, they hesitated—everyone knows that southern bounty hunters fear dead bodies and ghosts—but only for a moment. Gregg and Steve, inside the crypt with the family, listened in terror as the bounty hunters pounded and tugged on the door. But just then a huge black snake hissed and struck at the leader, sinking fangs deep into the flesh of his wrist and crunching bone. The scoundrels fled in panic with their dogs howling behind them. The next morning, the boys helped the family get to the next station on the freedom trail, a farm in Warwick.

It was a good story. The boys spent several weeks revisiting the crypt and beehive, looking for the secret tunnel. The stone floor of the crypt made a hollow sound when they struck it with a stick, but the stones were too heavy for them to lift. I always found some excuse for not aiding them in their search for the tunnel while appreciating the clues they found confirming its existence. New stories followed, taking the children off on different adventures while the secret tunnel faded from memory. My kids grew up, left home, and the stories ended.

About twenty-five years later, I was surprised one misty Sunday morning to see a group of eight to ten people standing around the door to the crypt. Several had cameras, and others were taking notes as a balding man in a red wool shirt was giving some sort of discourse. When I walked over to greet them, I discovered they were a group of history buffs, members of the New England Antiquities Research Association on a Sunday tour of historical sites in Wendell and New Salem. The crypt was on their list. They asked me what I knew about its history.

I opened the crypt and let them enter. They listened attentively while I told them what I had learned about the history of the crypt, mostly from Susie Bean's story and some subsequent research. They were very interested and several took pictures and made notes in their journals.

As I was leaving, one of the group came up to me and confidentially asked me if I knew that the house and crypt had once been part of the Underground Railroad. He went on to tell me of a tunnel that had been dug from the house to the crypt, and how, one night, runaway slaves had escaped pursuing bounty hunters by using the tunnel and hiding in the crypt. The only thing he missed was the big black snake.

My story had come home.

Proven Volunteer Support throughout the North Quabbin

Joe Hawkins

The North Quabbin towns have long been unique because people always come together in support of any person or group of people in need. This optimism is evident in the never-ending generosity offered in money and volunteerism necessary to support organizations such as Athol Hospital (formerly Athol Memorial Hospital) and the Athol Area YMCA. It has long been assumed that the size and population base of our area could never support a hospital or a YMCA, but people of North Quabbin have time and again proven they can support such organizations simply because of their importance and vital necessity to our area. The Athol Lions Club and Rotary Club of the Athol-Orange Area are two excellent examples of members continually working toward the betterment of our communities.

I was privileged to be the executive director of the Athol Area YMCA for thirty-eight years, beginning in 1971. The Y for the North Quabbin was founded in 1859. The present building was built in 1911 on land donated by Laroy S. Starrett, founder of the L. S. Starrett Company, a world-renowned manufacturer of precision tools. The Y building was renovated and greatly enlarged in 1971. Prior to the expansion, Alexander P. (Johnnie) Johnstone led the Y for more then fifty years.

The Y has always been and will continue to be "The Purposeful Community Center." The great motto of the Y and indeed its obsessive purpose is to "build strong kids, strong families, and strong communities." YMCAs offer values-oriented programming with emphasis on the physical, beginning at six months of age and for youth, adults, and older adults eighty and even ninety years of age or older. Along with the great array of program offerings, the board of directors and Y staff knew that with the expanded facilities, more could be done for the people in our communities.

As times and needs change, the Y always attempts to meet the challenges through its own resources. The Y strives to encourage and promote change in concert with other organizations and even aid in creation of relevant groups or needed agencies.

Many Ys in other communities have chosen not to include men's residence in their facilities. Recognizing the vital need served, our Y has purposely kept twenty apartments for men. Hundreds or even thousands of men have had the opportunity for affordable living quarters while in transition. Toward this end, the Athol Area Y contracted with Massachusetts Housing and Shelter Alliance (MHSA) to use six apartments for men who are temporarily homeless and willing and able to work and seek housing. The program staff meets regularly with each man to guide him toward permanent housing, employment, and techniques for managing finances.

In the late 1970s, there was a tremendous need throughout the country for work force development. The Community Employment Training Act (CETA) became law. Franklin County-North Quabbin Area CETA requested facility space at the Y. CETA developed programs for youth to work after school at nonprofit organizations. It also started employment programming for youth who had dropped out of school with the expectation that they would participate in GED High School Diploma classes. Full time summer youth employment served more then 150 youth in this area. Unemployed adult work programs were initiated in cooperation with private industry and organizations that would hire these individuals following a year of supplemental funding.

The CETA program ended in the early 1980s, but other agencies continued to receive funding for work placement and adult computer training through the year 2000 in the Y facilities. Such programs continue in other various facilities throughout Franklin and Hampshire Counties—with North Quabbin participants.

The Y donated initial space to a self-help effort which encouraged simple bartering between individuals, families, and small business endeavors. This grew into the Community Development Corporation for self-help in larger building and housing projects and for searching out special funding sources.

The Y continues to work with area schools. After-school programs such as Athol Comes Together in Our Neighborhoods (ACTION) was organized for fifth and sixth graders. This program was held in school after regular hours, with teachers and Y staff working cooperatively with thirty at-risk students. A middle school arts and activities program is held each afternoon at the Y. Community Transit Service donates daily school-to-Y busing for those students who wish to participate. The middle school and the Y work hand in hand to present the Multi

Cultural Festival evening held at the school annually each June. There has been a dual effort between middle school teachers and the Y staff to promote basic values regarding daily life situations.

In 1985, the Area Health Education Center of the University of Massachusetts was researching what resources were available to communities, and more specifically to the population in need. The researchers discovered that there were many active and excellent agencies and services available, but they were not connecting with each other. And, unbelievably many were not aware of other resources. With this realization came the most unique and meaningful collaborative effort for this area, which is, in fact, a national model for social agency cooperation and effectiveness. The North Quabbin Community Coalition (NQCC), was born. The Y devoted a small space to the initial effort toward this collaboration of the Coalition for information and referral. This fledgling agency took calls and began to disseminate requests and needs to the proper resources. The Coalition next invited all area social agency representatives to meet regularly each month, initially in the YMCA conference area. Gradually thirty and sometimes up to fifty people would come together in participation. Town officials and our state legislators, both representatives and senators, attended. Occasionally the governor and even US representatives attended. This forum saw very little "turf fighting." Mutual understanding and cooperation grew, always with the ever present optimism of the agencies and their participants. It soon became obvious that families and individuals had not one need but several which could be addressed by agencies working together. The coalition is the uniting force bringing social agencies, towns, schools, businesses, and legislators to the table. This true cooperative venue epitomizes the wonderful uniqueness of the communities and people of the North Quabbin. Although often taken for granted, the North Quabbin Community Coalition is unique in its effectiveness; we are fortunate to have this unduplicated model.

Due to the impact on our communities, a major funding foundation approached our area to develop a project that would affect families for future generations. Valuing Our Children (VOC) started with the director visiting literally hundreds of households asking for input. The result was many parents, never before contacted, getting involved as participants as well as trainers for parent and family betterment programs. VOC found great value initially being headquartered at the Y due to its reputation as a values-oriented agency in the area. This organization is a non-judgmental parenting and child abuse prevention venture. It positively affects hundreds of families now and for future generations.

Previous to 1983 there were separate annual local fund drives for the Girl Scouts, Boy Scouts, the American Red Cross, Salvation Army and the YMCA. It made great sense to bring these vital organizations together for one annual financial campaign. The YMCA donated office space to the United Way, not only because of its importance to the Y, but also to the other agencies—with Literacy Volunteers being added only a few years after its inception.

The United Way continues to aid in the work of these agencies due to the optimistic and generous support of the people and businesses in the North Quabbin.

The North Quabbin is unique due to the cooperative networking of almost all social agencies, clubs, businesses, schools, town officials, state representatives, and most importantly, the generosity and optimism of the people in these communities. It doesn't hurt that the beauty and natural resources of this area are unsurpassed.

Hands across North Quabbin

Phil Rabinowitz

For Dave Flint, HANDS started with the Goth kids at the Independence Day celebration. When they came walking up the street with their piercings and strange haircuts, Dave, in charge of setting up and running the event for the Lions Club, said to himself, "Here comes trouble." But they paid for their tickets and there was no excuse for keeping them out. Dave picks up the story:

"The day started off warm and sunny, but later in the afternoon, a huge thunderstorm came up. The wind was blowing like crazy, and it really looked like the tents were going to come down. We were all running every which way trying to keep anyone from getting hurt. And who was right in the middle of everything, holding up tent poles and calming people down, but those kids. And I said to myself, 'You judged those kids based on what you thought they were like, and you were dead wrong.' And I decided I just wouldn't do that anymore."

Hands Across North Quabbin, known as HANDS, is an organization that exists to foster collaboration across differences in the nine-town North Quabbin region. Its purpose is to help the region become, and become known as, the most collaborative area in Massachusetts, making it an ideal place to live and work. The real difference in its approach is that it aims directly at changing the culture of the region so that the norm becomes one of all citizens, regardless of their differences, working together to solve problems and address issues in ways that are both effective and acceptable to the vast majority of the population.

The nine-town North Quabbin region is a sparsely populated rural area in the midst of one of the most densely populated states in the country; an area that tracks center-right in one of the most politically liberal states in the country; and an area that has been marked by both exceptional collaboration and intense polarization. While North Quabbin residents regularly band together to help neighbors in trouble—when there's a house fire or serious illness, for instance--they have also in the past been at one another's throats over sensitive issues. One of the region's three school systems was essentially paralyzed for years because of a dysfunctional and factionalized school committee, for example. In another town, controversy raged over proposed budget-driven layoffs of municipal employees.

While the region's population is almost entirely white, it is diverse in nearly every other way, encompassing differences of age, class, politics, education, economic status, ethnicity, and religion, to name only some. At a time of particularly intense polarization in the early two-thousands, a group of collaborative-minded people—human service workers, Lions Club members (including Dave, who told the story at the beginning of this piece), area clergy, and others—founded the Institute for Community Building (ICB) in order to foster trust and understanding across those lines of difference.

Although ICB had some successes at bringing people together, it became clear to Mark Shoul, the group's former director and moving force, that it wasn't getting at the root causes of the polarization that made it difficult to address serious economic and other issues facing the region. With that in mind, Shoul assembled a network of respected community members, including ICB board members and others, to work more specifically on building collaboration among individuals and groups in the North Quabbin by helping them start and carry out collaborative projects. That network became HANDS.

Over the course of the next few years, HANDS experimented with different approaches. It considers itself a learning network, continually seeking out ways to engage the region's residents in addressing issues and to shift the culture in the direction of collaboration. Most important, it strives to understand how to nurture the conditions that foster collaboration.

Among these conditions seem to be:

A network of respected community members who can both model and spread the spirit and behavior of collaboration.

The building of familiarity and trust among diverse groups, particularly those who might not have much contact. That familiarity and trust can lead to the formation of social capital, the web of expectations and obligations that binds individuals and groups together in a community or society.

Community members' expectation that if they engage in attempting to address an issue or solve a problem, others will engage as well, and that there will be a reasonable chance of success.

The expectation that everyone will act in a civil and reasonable way, even when there are deep disagreements, and that conflict can be resolved if everyone is committed to collaboration.

HANDS is hardly the only organization that tries to build collaboration, but it is unusual in that it doesn't sponsor or run programs. Rather, its purpose is to act as a catalyst, an agent that makes a chemical reaction possible even though the catalyst itself doesn't change. HANDS operates in that way, bringing together people who are interested in addressing an issue or accomplishing a goal. Its intent is to help them to clarify what they want to do and how to do it and to aid them to form a network or organization to do the job, while not itself being part of or overseeing their efforts.

This overall approach—focusing on culture, changing the underlying conditions to those conducive to collaboration, catalyzing but not spearheading community activity—is different and effective enough that HANDS was chosen in 2009 as one of only twenty winners out of five thousand applicants of a Case Foundation grant recognizing innovative ideas for increasing the active involvement of citizens in addressing their community's toughest issues. Case also wrote up HANDS as an exemplary program in its final report on the grant competition.

These are some of the community efforts that HANDS, often working with other groups, has catalyzed over the past several years:

The building of a pavilion at Silver Lake in Athol, overseen and accomplished through the efforts of the Athol Lions Club, and dedicated to the memory of Dick Phillips, a Lion and Athol resident whose life exemplified the philosophy of collaboration across differences in service to the community.

A successful effort to resolve a crisis in the Athol-Royalston Regional School District when the high school lost accreditation. This effort brought together diverse members of the community and ultimately resulted in the restoration of accreditation, a high school library/media center built with volunteer labor and donated materials, and a strategic plan for the district.

The North Quabbin Green Economy Network, which grew out of a community forum convened by HANDS to identify areas that community members wanted to work on. The Network applied for and received a grant from the state to explore environmental improvements in seven towns, and resulted in Green Community designations for three of the seven. It also brought millions of dollars of investment in green, particularly solar, technology to the area.

A collaboration with the Athol Area YMCA that brought a new, participant-run program for teens at the Y.

The Forgiveness Project, a community art project based on Martin Luther King's concept of forgiveness as "not an individual act, but a permanent attitude." Launched in collaboration with the area's annual Martin Luther King Day celebration, the project will bring a spiral "Forgiveness Walk," designed by local artist Mary King, to Butterfield Park in Orange.

A current collaboration with the Athol Area YMCA and the Athol-Royalston Regional School District to garner community support for making the district a symbol of excellence in education for the state. This collaboration has yielded three well-attended community meetings, commitments from community members and businesses to provide specific kinds of support, and the first steps of a new five-year strategic plan to replace the last one, which has run its five-year course.

In each of these projects, HANDS has helped to put together groups of collaborators and acted as initial convener but has stepped back (or will step back, in the case of ongoing efforts) as groups gained momentum and began to function on their own. Its concern is not individual projects: those have been and can be carried out and sustained by groups of interested community members. The goal of HANDS is to change the culture to the point that every North Quabbin resident, when faced with a community issue or problem, immediately asks him- or herself, "Who is affected by this, who needs to be involved in resolving it, and how can we collaborate to make all our lives better?" This is a long-term process that will require continued effort over an extended period, but the organization's success to date shows that it can be accomplished. HANDS is in it for the long run.

Village School Reading Buddies read their poems and share related drawings with other classes as the culmination of the All School Poetry Project.

The Village School in Royalston

Rise Richardson

Wander over to Royalston Common during the school year, and you might find a class of children in the woods engaged in a tree study, another class rehearsing its annual play outside, and another class on its way to the Phineas Newton Royalston library. You have chanced upon the Village School, an independent elementary school on Royalston Common.

In the late 1960s and early 1970s, John G. Bennett, philosopher, scientist, and educator, founded the International Academy for Continuous Education in England for post-college and older adults. The academy taught practical ways to bring balance to human development. By employing methods to develop and integrate the emotional life and the life of the physical body, Bennett addressed overemphasis on development of the intellect in modern education. He also taught methods to develop attention, using it as a key instrument in the learning process.

Bennett felt strongly that much difficulty of modern life stems from disconnection to nature, so as part of the educational program, students worked in the garden, learned forestry, and in the process, learned how to become centered within themselves.

Many of Bennett's students were American and came back to the US where they lived in the Boston area. Over time and seeking a more rural life, a number of them settled in the beautiful, quiet North Quabbin area. They decided to create an educational model for their children to provide balance missing from their own childhood.

In the spring of 1989, this group of parents incorporated as Millers River Educational Cooperative, Inc. and began the Village School preschool at the Morgan Memorial Camp in South Athol. They welcomed parents and children from the nearby community. As the school grew, influences from Maria Montessori, Elizabeth Bennett, A.L. Stavely, Waldorf education, and other systems of pedagogy were integrated into the curriculum. Music, art, fairy tales, and fostering a strong sense of community addressed the emotional life. Physical challenges served the physical body. The curriculum included direct contact with nature. Each year, another grade was added, eventually through sixth grade.

Eventually, Millers River Educational Cooperative purchased Camp Caravan property in Royalston for the site of the future home for the Village School, for summer programs, and as a campus for practical adult education. In the same year, the Village School moved into the Raymond School building on Royalston Common.

At the Village School, an overall theme connects areas of study in the pre-school and K-through-sixth-grade curricula. Themes are chosen based on an understanding of children's development: younger children are focused on the immediate world around them and older children are beginning to explore the larger world, both in the present and times past. A typical theme for K-1 children might be rocks and minerals for three or four months. Older children may spend a whole year exploring Ancient Greece. Threads from the theme sew together all academic areas including writing, reading, science, math, and others. Areas such as art and music bring hands-on theme enhancement.

Every classroom works on building community, especially at the start of the school year and using *Responsive Classroom* techniques. Classes begin the day with a morning meeting and often end the day with a finishing meeting when children and adults share personal experiences and triumphs and failures. Older children are reading buddies with younger children and read to them once a week. They pair together for school events. Because of reading buddies, older children look out for younger children in the playground. You can often see a K-6 soccer game at recess.

The fully integrated curriculum includes reading, writing, and oral language. The approach fosters a love for reading and writing with daily exposure to poems, stories, songs, non-fiction, and journal- and story-writing. Students learn to read through daily experiences with literature. They learn from the beginning that they are authors: their journals comprise an integral part of the day. They write their own stories using pictures, dictation, and best-choice spelling according to age level. As children grow older, they learn to incorporate more formal writing skills into their stories and essays.

The math curriculum helps children to understand underlying mathematical concepts and patterns while developing flexibility and competence in computational skills. Experience with concrete materials provides an opportunity to explore computational concepts.

Manipulatives include unifix cubes, pattern blocks, base ten blocks, coins, rods and geoboards.

The science program focuses on observation and study of the natural world, taking advantage of the rural location of the Village School. The Village School science program touches upon subjects in all the major scientific disciplines every year. Activities in biology, chemistry, physics, earth science, and space science are offered in every classroom. Children in the fourth through sixth grades enthusiastically explore, research and present their own science projects each spring, without parent help.

Visual arts as well as music, movement, dance, drama, and storytelling all take place as a regular part of classroom activities and are given as much priority as other curriculum areas. The arts also form a rich component of the thematic studies.

A mixed-age classroom offers wonderful opportunities for children to learn from each other. Children of different levels help each other master new skills. Older children have a chance to reinforce newly mastered skills by teaching younger ones. Children learn at different speeds, and the mixed-age group classroom allows for a great deal of flexibility; children who are gifted in a certain skills are allowed to move ahead, while still being able to socialize with children their own age. Those who need extra help can learn a skill with a younger group while still socializing with age peers. The range of ages promotes acceptance of various levels of competence, helps children assume responsibility for each other, and results in a number of satisfying cross-age friendships.

The Village School has an ongoing relationship with the Farm School, Sweetwater Farm, and Richardsons' Farm. All classes visit these farms during the school year and work during the visits all day in the natural rhythm of a farm. Students develop relationships with animals, staff, and special places on the farms. Students are able to follow the flow of farm life throughout the seasons, throughout the year, and throughout the years.

The Village School offers an after school program and summer programs for children in the North Quabbin region.

A capital campaign is in full swing to build a permanent home for the Village School on the old fifty-five acre Camp Caravan property in

Royalston. At the new campus, children will be able to feed chickens, visit sheep, go on forest walks, work in an art studio, participate in dance classes, and more.

Some sixty children are enrolled at the Village School, from preschool through the sixth grade. Families are encouraged to explore the school as a choice for their child's education. Go to the website www.villageschoolma.org for information about the admissions process. The Village School has a strong financial aid program with the aim of having a diverse group of families at the school. The school community is an inclusive village, and graduates have a lifetime connection to this village and return often to visit.

With Tom Musco and Deborah D'Amico of Royalston Oak, Village Schoolers built a model timber-frame house in the Village School driveway, above. Village School second and third graders don Colonial garb for Colonial Dress-Up Day as part of their year-long study of Colonial America, top, next page; Village School pre-schoolers costume themselves for Halloween, bottom, next page.

Ricky Baruc and Deb Habib nurtured the dream of Seeds of Solidarity on Chestnut Hill Road in Orange while preparing for a 1994 pilgrimage from Auschwitz to Hiroshima organized by Leverett's New England Peace Pagoda. Once they established Seeds of Solidarity, they and neighbors created the renowned harvest-time North Quabbin Garlic & Arts Festival.

Seeds of Solidarity

Deb Habib

We decided on the name Seeds of Solidarity before we'd even seen, let alone moved to, Chestnut Hill Road in Orange. It was 1994, and my soul mate Ricky Baruc and I were preparing to embark on the Interfaith Pilgrimage for Peace and Life from Auschwitz to Hiroshima, an eight-month walk commemorating the fiftieth anniversary of the end of World War II as well as visit places of current conflict in the former Yugoslavia, Israel, Palestine, and Iraq. Conceived by the Japanese monks and nuns of Nipponzan Myohoji as part of their Buddhist social activism, the seed to join was planted while Ricky volunteered his carpentry skills on their Peace Pagoda temple in Leverett, near where we were then living. We were deeply called to the purpose of the walk itself and also knew we might at times diverge to connect with other farmers. We had been farming (Ricky) and engaged in agriculture education (Deb) since young interns at the New Alchemy Institute on Cape Cod, which is also where we met and fell in love in 1984. As we prepared for the next phase of our life together—marriage, the pilgrimage, then a vision for our future farm together—we recalled a sign we had made for our very first market garden together while at New Alchemy: "This garden is grown in solidarity with those around the world helping to feed the people."

Truth be told, that early conversation about the name turned into a bit of a marital argument. Ricky insisted we didn't need to have acquired the land to name and evolve the vision; I countered that it didn't exist until, well, it existed. He was right. The seed of a strong vision was planted and began to germinate from its conception. And to this day, the under use of the word "solidarity" in the lexicon of mainstream conversation often creates opportunity for explanation. Often, I'm asked to spell out the word when on the phone with various customer service agents or governmental representatives. My favorite was when I said Seeds of Solidarity, and they repeated back what they'd thought they'd heard: "Caesar Salad-arity?"

But back to the story. Upon return to Massachusetts from the pilgrimage in 1995, we found ourselves led by the desire to find affordable land and a distaste for "land-as-commodity" real estate mentality. We wanted to become conservation buyers (ultimately among the first with an agricultural rather than forested land focus) from Mount Grace Land Conservation Trust, then a relatively new and very small organization with Leigh Youngblood at its helm. We wanted to be in a community where there was need and we could be of service. We didn't want to, and in fact could never have afforded to, be in the heart of the Pioneer Valley. At the time, we didn't even really think much about neighbors or schools—just some affordable land where we could plant seeds we'd carried back from Turkey, India, Israel, and Vietnam as well as vegetables for market. We could bring people to learn to grow food. We could build a home with enough solar exposure to live off the electric utility grid, a commitment strengthened by our visit to Iraq where we witnessed firsthand the human and ecological devastation of wars over oil.

With our initial focus on the land itself, we could never have known how deeply we would, twenty years later, unconventional ideas and all, become immersed in and welcomed into the community. We began working the soil with no-till organic practices on ground that was so poor for crops that people said we'd never grow anything. Little by little, we built the soil using local resources like manure from area farms and mostly layer upon layer of cardboard and mulch to open and enrich the land, follow nature's lead, and feed the life in the soil without the use of mechanization. While many think this way of farming is unique, in fact only two percent of the world's farmers use machinery. The rest use animal power and, primarily, their hands. There are hundreds of farming stories from those early years: Ricky racing out in the middle of a torrential downpour to access water for the greenhouse before we had a functioning well while, hoping he wouldn't be struck by lightning, I waited inside with a newborn. Or the years of young farm apprentices we hosted who ran the spectrum from wacky to wonderful.

Bringing people to the land and extending our methods out to the community was a priority from the start, and working with local young people topped our list. My doctoral research on teenagers engaged in environmental issues in their communities confirmed my faith in the power of youthful changemakers. Plus enough time spent in academia—through a self-shaped and circuitous path of my own education as well as teaching—confirmed I did not want to be there. After an exploratory year of Seeds of Leadership (SOL) Garden for local teenagers, we embarked on officially founding Seeds of Solidarity Education Center, Inc., a nonprofit 501c3 organization.

A short article is not enough to share the dreams and despair, exhilaration and exhaustion that characterize running a small non-profit organization, but I would not have it any other way. Our flagship youth program had operated for seventeen seasons at this writing, with more than 350 local young people having cultivated food and a hopeful future and many lives, including ours, profoundly impacted. We've launched and sustained a number of other initiatives over the years to celebrate and make visible Seeds of Solidarity's mission to "awaken the power of youth, schools, and families to Grow Food Everywhere to transform hunger to health and create resilient lives and communities."

Seeds of Solidarity gardens nourish patients at area hospitals and students in local schools and visitors to the community health center. We feed residents through raised beds that grace the entrance at our local library, a converted factory, the food pantry, our new community food co-op, and for ten (and counting) family childcare providers to teach young ones in their care to grow, prepare, and enjoy fresh food.

Yes, these are made possible through our food growing skills and those of our small staff, but more so through partnerships that we have worked to create and an amazing region filled with resourceful and wise people as well as those with great life struggles, who have watched, applauded, and participated in ideas that are often pretty outside the box.

Among the grandest of the "who'da thunk it" ideas is the North Quabbin Garlic and Arts Festival. Sometimes people who visit on our Solidarity Saturday tours ask if we ever thought about living in community, meaning an intentional or co-housing community. "We do," we reply, "It's called a neighborhood." Early on in our time here, 1998 to be exact, Ricky (who was growing ample garlic) was having a conversation with neighbor and Athol native Jim Fountain, a talented woodworker. Lamenting the lack of local venues for farmers and artists, they conceived the idea for a regional festival. Over a potluck dinner, five neighbors, Jim and wife Alyssa, artist and neighbor Lydia Grey, and Ricky and I— brainstormed a vision of a homegrown, quality, family-friendly event. We each put twenty dollars in the middle of the table and set the date for the first annual North Quabbin Garlic and Arts Festival to take place one year later in September of 1999.

The Festival, which we fondly publicize as "The Festival that Stinks," attracts ten thousand people to the fields of Forster's Farm in Orange each year in a community that, when we first arrived here, the *Boston Globe* almost gleefully berated for its "economic and social demise." In these times of excessive technology and corporate control of food and entertainment, people are searching for authentic experiences that touch the heart and soul. In addition to the truly fine artists, farmers, chefs, performers, and educational experiences, it is the sense of community at the essence of the event that people feel and that brings them back. Now an organizing group of fifteen with more than two hundred community volunteers the weekend of the festival—intentionally without a hierarchical structure or corporate sponsors—is a self-sustaining event important to the livelihood of a hundred regional farmers, artists, and food producers. It ignites the local business and tourism economy. Plus, the event has been able to give more than twenty thousand dollars in grants to other organizations to spread the spirit of community building year round.

It has been two decades since we coined Seeds of Solidarity and set out to grow, in more ways than one. Our friends from the Valley no longer ask why we would possibly move to Orange.

We are grateful every day for the land that nourishes our relationship, our family and community, for our amazing neighbors and support that surrounds us, and for the incredible beauty and resilience to be found here.

In 2013, the North Quabbin Garlic & Arts Festival celebrated its fifteenth anniversary.

Quabbin Harvest

Marcia Gagliardi

"The only way this is going to work," declares Amy Borezo of Orange, chair of Quabbin Harvest, North Quabbin's cooperative food market, "is if people come in to the store to shop. *That's* how we'll be here in twenty years."

Borezo's assessment occurs in August, 2014, on the cusp of opening the food coop's fifteen-hundred-square-foot retail space in the former Workers' Credit Union building on North Main Street, Orange, then next to the Bohemian Kitchen restaurant that closed in March, 2015. Mount Grace Land Conservation Trust acquired the building with the coop in mind, and Quabbin Harvest rents the space from the land trust.

Donated commercial refrigerators, freezers, fixtures, and labor augment purchased store necessities on the first floor, and pleasant, freshly-painted murals adorn the walls. The floor is new, and all vestiges of the former bank have been erased. An open second-floor area serves as a community room.

Borezo and coop executive committee colleagues Julie Davis, merchandising coordinator; Robin Shtulman, recent past board secretary; and Nina Wellen, treasurer, do not contain their enthusiasm nor affection for one another as they field questions about Quabbin Harvest, an enterprise that has been their passion since they cooked it up in neighborly conversation along about 2009.

All transplants to the North Quabbin, the four women whose ages hover around the forties share intelligence, humor, dedication, and most importantly vision with the almost three hundred coop members they led at the time of the coop's opening. They emphasize that five other board members and some eighty volunteers have collaborated diligently and extensively to make Quabbin Harvest a reality.

"If you want something to happen around here," observes Shtulman, who grew up in the New York City Borough of Queens, "you have to do it yourself. When I first moved here, I thought it was a drawback, but then I realized it's a strength. We wanted this coop, and we had to make it happen."

Laughter from her friends approves Shtulman's observation. "None of us had community when we moved here," adds Davis, whose

Board members and manager of the Quabbin Harvest food cooperative in Orange display a tote bag proclaiming the coop logo. They are, from left, Julie Davis, Nina Wellen, Robin Shtulman, Julie Robinson, and Amy Borezo. Neighbors Davis, Wellen, Shtulman, and Borezo—all transplants to the North Quabbin—decided that the area needed a food coop. With many other volunteers, they created one.

hometown is Hopedale, Massachusetts. "But when you get here, you will find your group. This coop has succeeded because everyone's personal skills have meshed."

"I was sort of despairing about finding community when I got here," says Wellen, whose roots are in the Westchester County, New York, town of Chappaqua. "At first, I couldn't find a reflection of my values. Everyone works, and it was hard to find people to do things with. It's important for us to create something. And then I found this group and the will to make this coop happen."

"Our values cross the spectrum of so many people," states Borezo, who hails from Louisiana and Georgia. "We are working so hard at this because we want it to happen. We want people to be comfortable in the coop and provide good food at prices that treat our members and customers right."

"We have incredible community support," concludes Shtulman. "People want us to succeed."

Banter, camaraderie, and enthusiasm can not disguise the years of thought, planning, and sheer hard work the executive committee members have contributed to fruition of their earlier dream for a retail food coop—a place that seems a little like a supermarket in the center of Orange: a supermarket dedicated conscientiously to selling wholesome, carefully-selected food grown locally or made caringly.

The grown locally part figures essentially into Quabbin Harvest's game plan. Early on, the coop developed caring, mutually respectful relationships with North Quabbin farmers. Seeds of Solidarity's transplants-to-the-North-Quabbin Deb Habib and Ricky Baruc, with others at the heart of the annual garlic festival, and Orange farmers Laura and John Moore, direct descendant of a founder of the town of Orange, early on endorsed the coop.

Davis underscores the importance of the coop's relationship with local farmers. "Every week, they provide our produce shares," she says. "You can't imagine how supportive the farmers are. I'm excited to show people what exists in our area. We have reached out to twenty farmers over the years, and they have responded amazingly. I can call them to see what's available for shares, and they discuss our needs with me. Next year, some of them are going to grow crops specifically for the coop. It's mutually beneficial."

Julie Robinson, coop manager, came on board in June, 2014. "It was kismet," she says. "I knew it was *my* job the minute I saw it posted. I said I *have* to have this job. I put everything in to being totally me. I already knew my vision."

A native of Arlington, Massachusetts, Robinson's experience with coops extends from her stint with the Arlington coop, years with Northeast Cooperative, the Concord Coop in New Hampshire, and the Brattleboro, Vermont, Coop where she most recently worked for six years.

"I was so impressed at the interview with Julie R," says Davis. "I thought she speaks with authority and already she says 'we.'"

Clearly, Robinson's style and manner fit with the coop executive committee of friends who hired her. Walking through the soon-to-be store as yet fitted only with several large coolers and a freezer,

Robinson lovingly creates the intended layout in detail from memory for an observer. "And that mural on the wall represents our wonderful surroundings, the North Quabbin with its hills and water and earth. And the floor represents the earth and water, the beautiful Quabbin Reservoir. I am so happy to be here."

The coop began on the grounds of the Orange Innovation Center under a tent with produce and weekly community-supported agriculture shares offered for sale. "Then it got cold," said Borezo, "and we wondered what to do."

"We had no overhead then," adds Davis.

"And we had no debt," Borezo says.

They leased a 250-square-foot unheated space at OIC to continue operation during the winter. "Our volunteers sat with fingerless gloves and hats and jackets inside in order to sort the shares," remembers Wellen.

"And then we had overhead," Borezo says. "We had to pay the rent. We had to pay the electricity bill. We began to have financial obligations. But still we had no debt. We struggled, finally, with the decision to put a one-thousand-dollar freezer on a credit card. We are fiscally very conservative. We want our investors to benefit from the coop."

Member-investors post $120 for a lifetime membership and ante up each week the price of any share they want to buy. Separately, they and the public can purchase food in the coop store. "We want it to be very, very clear that everyone is welcome in the store," chorus the women. "We want to welcome our friends and neighbors, and we want to carry the food they want."

"We already have Dean's Beans Coffee and Chase Hill Farm cheese," says Wellen.

"I remember when I drove miles and miles to find fresh, good food," Borezo says wistfully. "To the Valley. To Greenfield. But not now. Now I know where to find it right here in the North Quabbin."

Those who want to be members can pick up forms at the Quabbin Harvest store. Detailed information about the coop is available online at nqeats.org along with opportunities to buy a weekly produce share or membership (including a four-payment plan of thirty dollars a month for four months).

photo by Michael Skillicorn

Among scores of volunteers who transformed the former Workers Credit Union building into a lively food cooperative market are Mary-Ann and Tony Palmieri, above, of New Salem.

Other board members are Karl Bittenbender, Manuel King, Mary King, Shane Peters, and Michael Skillicorn, who recently accepted the position of secretary when Shtulman stepped down.

"We're lucky our families are supportive of what we do," said Davis. "We're out of our homes an awful lot on coop business, but our families know it's all for this great enterprise."

"You know what?" says Shtulman, looking around the community room. "We should have a big, big party up here. Wouldn't that be fun? We can look out these windows at the town below and just have a blast."

In the meantime, the exuberant cohort with its board and volunteers seems already to be having a blast working hard and creating their own good time.

DeDe Johnson's coffee cake, top left, earned her a finalist's position in the General Mills Foodservice Neighborhood to Nation Recipe Contest. DeDe, top right, owns Johnson's Farm Restaurant and Sugar House on Wheeler Avenue in Orange with her husband, Steve.

Johnson Farm's DeDe Johnson: General Mills Contest Finalist

Courtesy of *Athol Daily News*

Residents of the North Quabbin region know the quality, homemade food served at Johnson's Farm. That knowledge went national with DeDe Johnson being named one of three finalists in the General Mills Foodservice first Neighborhood to Nation Recipe Contest, in which "neighborhood" restaurants across the nation were invited to submit a dish that reflects a local flavor for a chance to put their local dish in the national spotlight.

It is the first time she has ever entered any kind of contest, Johnson explains, but one day an invitation to submit an entry came in the mail and she decided to give it a try.

The rules of the contest were simple enough, submit a recipe that uses at least one product made by General Mills - which includes brands like Pillsbury, Gold Medal, Nature Valley and Yoplait - and Johnson ended up using two. Armed with a cookbook from the Bethany Lutheran Church that she estimates dates back to the 1970s, she began experimenting. "I drove everyone nuts trying recipes," she said, before settling on a recipe for Yogurt Chocolate Chip Coffee Cake, something she learned from a fellow member of the congregation and that has become a favorite at the restaurant. Normally she makes the dish from scratch, but because of the contest requirements she ended up using a coffee cake mix, the kind that you just add water to, and substituted the required sour cream with Yoplait yogurt, which she admits actually imparted a pleasant tangy taste to the coffee cake. Just for good measure though, she also submitted a recipe for maple walnut pancakes.

The recipes were submitted back in September, and Johnson said she has known for a while that she was a finalist but was asked by the company to keep it a secret until they could alert the media.

Just for being a finalist Johnson earned ten thousand dollars. "The three finalists in the first Neighborhood to Nation Recipe Contest truly represent the heart of their neighborhoods and communities," said Danielle Benson, associate channel manager for General Mills Foodservice. "In addition to revealing their winning recipes, we are honored to share their unique stories, which showcase the strong connection that local family restaurants play within their community."

Johnson said she was very excited but still could not believe it is true. Johnson's Farm is a family restaurant, sugarhouse and gift shop that is well known for its home-cooked meals made from only the freshest and highest quality ingredients—including the family's namesake maple syrup that they've been making for more than a hundred years.

When the Johnsons inherited the family farm and sugar house in the late1990s, the property did not have a restaurant. As the family explored different ways to keep it up, DeDe said they tried different things including running a vegetable stand where they sold everything from the family's syrup to homemade pies and jellies.

In 1999, they built the Johnson's Farm Restaurant that sits today in the middle of the picturesque farm. It is a short drive from nearby towns but draws many visitors, particularly on weekends, who want to enjoy the countryside and get a glimpse of wildlife such as deer that roam in the fields or the farm's very own donkey and horse.

The Johnsons started by selling only homemade ice cream at the restaurant, then soon added breakfast, lunch, and dinner to meet the growing demand for DeDe's home-style cooking. A self-taught cook and baker, DeDe makes all the recipes for the restaurant's menu that spans comfort foods like familiar breakfast favorites (pancakes, biscuits and gravy, and doughnuts) to soups, sandwiches, and burgers.

The restaurant also boasts a robust dinner menu with options such as pasta, meatloaf and steak as well as several specialty items that incorporate Johnson's Maple Syrup including Maple Glazed Chicken, Salmon and Scallops, and Maple BBQ Ribs.

Beyond serving its own customers, Johnson's Farm helps to feed the greater community each year at an annual Thanksgiving dinner they kicked off four years ago. DeDe said they wanted to offer a way to give back by hosting a "community" dinner where everyone is welcome at no cost. More than 350 attended the first year, and the event continues to grow, both with the number of people who come out as well as the level of support that Johnson's Farm has received from other area businesses and their own customers.

To qualify for the Neighborhood to Nation Recipe Contest, restaurants from around the country submitted their favorite original breakfast, entrée, or dessert recipes using at least one ingredient from General Mills' list of eligible products.

Dinner Theater at Johnson's Farm • Wheeler Avenue, Orange

Candace R. Curran

In the afterglow of an
electrical storm's force-field
five deer reveal themselves
first the stag
and then the others begin

throwing themselves together
great gladiators at play
the smallest a bright dog star
herding the constellation
in a field of changing light

When we rise from the porch
deer in mid-frolic
come to a standstill
begin modeling a masterpiece
Hudson River School

Sky lowers a see-through
beaded curtain of rain
Thunder and lightening
autograph and applaud
delivering a painting to life

shepherding at the forest's green door
four that disappear and a
gilded fawn caught between
not wanting to go and not wanting
to be left behind

Perpetuating a family business and employing strategies for compassion toward animals advised by Temple Grandin, Adams Farm slaughterhouse in Athol serves New England with time-honored, family-oriented practice.

photo by Marcia Gagliardi

Family-Run Adams Farm Slaughterhouse

Edward Maltby

Adams Farm is a family-run 128-acre farm and USDA slaughterhouse located at the top of the hill at 854 Bearsden Road, Athol, Massachusetts where, on a clear day, you can see Mount Greylock in the Berkshires and Mount Monadnock in New Hampshire. The Adams Farm facility is sixteen thousand square feet with a state-of-the-art livestock harvesting and processing operation including a livestock holding area designed by Dr. Temple Grandin, the world's leading authority on the humane handling of animals.

When fire totally destroyed their facility in December 2006, the Adams family decided to rebuild across the road from the old site and modernize operations by tripling the size of the facility. The family made the decision to work with Temple Grandin on facility design because of their commitment to providing the best possible humane, hygienic, clean, and professional services to livestock farmers in New England. Dr. Grandin is a world-renowned expert in the design of livestock handling facilities and professor of animal science at Colorado State University. She has been able to use her autistic sensitivity to animal behavior to design curved chute and race systems that are used worldwide to reduce stress on animals during handling.

The business and land are family owned and operated by the Adams Farm Slaughterhouse LLC, whose members are Beverly Mundell, her son, Richard Adams, and daughter, Noreen Heath Paniagua. Three generations of the family now work and manage operations at the slaughterhouse, farm, and retail store where the freshest meat can be purchased and a great lunch of a sandwich and chips can be had for only two dollars.

Hester Adams purchased the land that became Adams Farm in 1919. Hester Adam's son Lewis married Beverly Heath (now Mundell), and her name was added as an owner in the tradition of the family where the importance of the role women play has always been recognized. Beverly and Lewis started the slaughterhouse as an addition to their dairy farm in 1946 and expanded rapidly to meet local demand for their services. In 1972, just after another major expansion to the facility, Lewis died suddenly from a brain hemorrhage, leaving Beverly with five growing children aged eight to sixteen and an expanding family business. Upon the death of her husband, Beverly took over sole management of the farm and slaughterhouse. She continues to play an active role in the operation in 2015. In 1990, Beverly added her son Rick Adams's name as an owner of the farmland to continue the family tradition, with the operations owned by Beverly, her daughter Noreen and son Rick, and run with the support of Rick's daughter, Sydney, and Noreen's daughter, Chelsea.

Adams Farm serves the combined New England states, which rank second in the country for agricultural products sold directly to individuals for human consumption. With 27,950 farms in New England preserving more than four million acres of active farmland, there is an overwhelming need for a viable infrastructure for farmers who wish to market their products directly to the consumer. The Adams Farm has become a necessary part of the survival of more than three hundred family farms in New England that have come to rely on Adams's slaughtering and meat-processing in the marketing of their product. Since the redesign and expansion, the Adams Farm is the largest slaughterhouse in New England and provides the high level of service necessary for quality processing of meats, whether it is marketed as USDA Organic, Halal, Animal Welfare Approved, Natural, Kosher, Local, or USDA Certified.

The family has a long-term commitment to the Town of Athol, the North Quabbin, and the Quabbin Valley community and makes every effort to use local businesses to provide the many services needed to support Adams Farm's expanding business. Adams Farm has become one of the larger employers in Athol with an average of forty-five employees, ninety percent of whom live in Athol.

The Adams family has a long-term commitment to preserving the environment and protecting the natural habitat, and the commitment is reflected in their farming operations. In 2012, Adams Farm Slaughterhouse leased fifteen acres of its hillside pasture to be developed as a solar farm that became fully operational in November 2013. In 2013, Adams Farm invested in an eighty-five solar-panel system to heat hot water for plant operations. This and other investment by the family reflect commitment to the local community, dedication to operating as an environmentally sound green business, and an expectation that the Adams family business will continue to be an active part of the North Quabbin and Quabbin Valley.

Television Coverage for the North Quabbin at AOTV

Carol Courville

When I came to the North Quabbin for a job, I had many first impressions of this area. I remember thinking it was a beautiful part of the state. I found the people to be hard-working and very friendly. My opinion hasn't changed. It has only grown more secure.

I came to the North Quabbin twenty years ago for a new job. I was incredibly excited to be hired as executive director to start Athol-Orange Community Television, now known as AOTV. I grew up in Worcester only one hour away, but you would think it was a million miles, since this quiet little area was never on my radar. I didn't know much about small towns, and I have discovered over the years that they are much different from large cities.

Just before my arrival, the board of directors purchased an old Victorian home on South Main Street, but it wasn't ready for occupancy. I was given an office at the North Quabbin Chamber of Commerce for the first three months, working next to Chamber Executive Director Tom Kussy. People came to greet me and introduce themselves. What a wonderful experience. AOTV had a meet-and-greet at The Homestead Restaurant. Everyone signed the guest book, and there are many names listed of people I still work with today. AOTV's original board of directors started the tradition of AOTV's "working board" by exemplifying dedication and care for the organization.

The first months were spent ordering TV equipment, writing policies, and painting the Victorian home. I remember the people who came by to lend a hand. No one knew me, and AOTV wasn't even on the air yet, so who were these volunteers who couldn't do enough to help? I know those first few months solidified my overwhelming and humbling opinion of the volunteerism in the community.

It was a few months after my arrival, on a Friday, just before a three-day weekend, the oil tank was empty. I called Orange Oil Company for the first time and explained the situation. I was not authorized to sign a check and could not reach the treasurer. Orange Oil came and put a hundred gallons in the tank and trusted that we would pay the bill. I was in shock that they would come, but this was my introduction to the incredible business community in town. To this day, Orange Oil has been an AOTV sponsor.

Carol Courville, executive director of Athol-Orange Community Television, AOTV, works the camera during the annual fund-raising auction.

AOTV's first program aired March 23, 1995. Our first River Rat Race was done in April 1995. We had just gotten the cameras and hadn't even had a full training class. The production had two cameras, one at the beginning of the race and one at the end. There were no cell phones then. To communicate, we used a pager. The following week, an elderly resident came by to thank me because it was the first time in all her years in Athol she was able to see the beginning of the race. Flash forward to 2013 and the fiftieth anniversary of the River Rat Race. We had ten camera angles including eight stationary, one Skype from the lead boat, and one camera live from the helicopter. It was a dream I had since we started covering the race. AOTV was still providing coverage, but we always try to do more for the community. We were on the air for thirteen hours from the 5K Cheese Road Race to the Lions Club's fireworks. AOTV still has only two fulltime staff, and these TV productions could not be done without great volunteers.

AOTV's mission is to train residents how to make their own programs to provide responsible, diverse, and informative programming to viewers. I started teaching TV production classes and have trained more than six hundred people in the past twenty years, which is much more than our counterparts in other communities.

Volunteers started producing Athol and Orange selectboard meetings. AOTV must have some influence in the community, because for the first five years of airing the meetings, every incumbent selectman running for office lost his/her election.

Eleven years ago, the Food-a-thon was started with a simple idea, "to raise food and funds for the North Quabbin Food Pantries." In collaboration with WJDF Radio, we produce a twelve-hour telethon/radio-a-thon to get the word out. The project has raised $219,832 for its mission. There are more than 125 volunteers who contribute to the cause. They come from businesses, churches, organizations, and people off the street.

Volunteers for AOTV also volunteer for other organizations in town. It's the concept that seems to be passed from one generation to the next in the area. Many people don't have the money, so they donate their time. However, there are many people who will write a check and still do the legwork.

I've always loved the diversity of AOTV volunteers. Yes, there are different ages, genders, and races, but the ideological and economic diversity is what intrigues me. Without comment or prejudice, I love showing AOTV volunteers how to get their message out to the community. Everyone is welcome at AOTV, and everyone is respectful of another's point of view.

The idea of volunteerism has rubbed off on me. Over the years I have been a board member of Literacy Volunteers of Orange/Athol and have served on the Salvation Army Advisory Board. I am a board member of the North Quabbin Chamber of Commerce and Athol-Orange Rotary Club. AOTV and I have become an integral part of the community, and I am grateful every day to be part of the North Quabbin area.

To this day, I give speeches to other access centers and tell them what wonderful volunteers we have in this area. They cannot believe that we get more than 110 volunteers for the AOTV auction. The success of the station can only be attributed to the volunteers.

Since twenty years have passed, there are many years that merge together in my mind now. Many auctions and River Rat Races have come and gone, but AOTV and the volunteers have stayed steadfast. AOTV has been around long enough to have lost two of its original board members. It is important to acknowledge that their vision along with hard work and dedication continues. Other volunteers have decided to retire from AOTV and pass the baton to the next generation. We wish them well and are grateful for all their years of support.

This recent email from a past volunteer sums up the thoughts better than I can: "Hearing from you caused me to reflect on the blessing that God bestowed upon me in allowing me to experience life with beautiful people like you and the AOTV family."

AOTV volunteers Jason Praplaski and Bonnie Benjamin set up for a shoot on Main Street in Athol.

A rarity in the information business in the early twenty-first century,
Athol Daily News *serves the sixteen thousand or so households in the*
North Quabbin with a circulation of fifty-two hundred copies. Daily.
Only thirty-two other Massachusetts newspapers are dailies, and most
of them serve medium- or large-sized cities. The United States supports
slightly more than thirteen hundred daily newspapers. That's an average
of about thirty-five daily newspapers per state (making Massachusetts
more or less typical). The population of the North Quabbin represents
a smaller readership area than most readership areas in the country.
Advertising revenue supports the news staff. Athol Daily News *qualifies*
as a remarkable and rare survivor in an industry challenged by social
media, the Internet, and daily habits of potential readers. It is one of the
more unique features of the North Quabbin.

North Quabbin Newspaper Coverage at Athol Daily News

Deb Porter

ATHOL—The *Athol Daily News*, this community's first daily newspaper, was founded eighty years ago by Lincoln O'Brien, son of a former editor of the *Boston Transcript* and *Boston Herald*. O'Brien was in his late twenties and an advertising manager for the *Beverly Evening Times* when he came to Athol. With little financial backing, he opened an office in the L. S. Starrett building on Main Street in quarters hurriedly made ready for newspaper use on the first floor and a section of the basement. He installed a press and other equipment and produced the first issue of the *Athol Daily News* on November 1, 1934.

The newspaper gained acceptance from townspeople, and less than a year later, the two remaining area weeklies, *Athol Transcript*, founded in 1871, and *Athol Chronicle*, dating from 1886, were absorbed by the *Athol Daily News*. In a span of ten months, the *Athol Daily News* became Athol's only newspaper. Before the end of its first year, circulation climbed to two thousand customers. O'Brien served as editor and publisher until he sold the newspaper to Edward T. Fairchild in 1941. Fairchild served as editor and publisher until he retired to Florida in the 1960s. Fairchild's son-in-law Richard J. Chase Sr. served as business manager and became a joint owner. When Fairchild retired, Chase became sole owner, president, and publisher in 1982.

A year later, his son Richard "Rick" Chase Jr. left a position at the Orange Savings Bank to join the paper as business manager, bringing a new generation on board. Rick Chase became president and general manager in 1988, then publisher in 1989 when the elder Chase retired.

The first news editor was Charles Cooke Jr., who died a hero during World War II. Barney Cummings served as editor for the next fifty years, retiring in 2010. Presently, Deborrah Porter is editor.

Today, the *Daily News* proudly serves the towns of Athol, Erving, Orange, New Salem, Petersham, Phillipston, Royalston, Warwick, and Wendell. Over the years, the business experienced a rapid evolution in the technology used to put out a newspaper. Overnight, the use of "hot type" gave way to a modern offset printing system.

Recent state-of-the-art upgrades to computer equipment, software, and cloud computing have further streamlined the process. And, unlike many other newspapers these days, the *Athol Daily News* prints each edition on site. The addition of two printing units aid with efficient production of color. The extra units allow the capacity of printing a sixteen-page paper with full color on the front and back pages.

The *Athol Daily News* has a website, www.atholdailynews.com, where subscribers may download full editions in PDF format directly to their computers, smart phones, and other mobile devices.

North Quabbin Radio Station WJDF

The North Quabbin region supports the radio station WJDF as well as the community television station AOTV and the Athol Daily News, *a daily newspaper.*

Beautiful Choral Music from Quabbin Valley Pro Musica

Mary-Ann DeVita Palmieri

When Quabbin Valley Pro Musica chorus performed an "Afternoon at the Opera" concert in Central Congregational Church in downtown Orange in winter, 2014, I was in charge of selling and collecting tickets. I was totally charmed by the concert but also by the reaction of the mostly local performers. Everyone was so appreciative that they were able to perform with such a professional group in their own North Quabbin area.

Charles Heffernan conducts Quabbin Valley Pro Musica, resident chorus of 1794 Meetinghouse, Inc.

photo by James Gilmour

For years the 1794 Meetinghouse Performing Arts Center has been presenting high quality performances in the Meetinghouse in New Salem, and one of its best and most successful endeavors has been its resident chorus, Quabbin Valley Pro Musica. Presently performing under the baton of Charles Heffernan, professor emeritus of music at UMass, Amherst, the chorus presents twice-yearly concerts in the summer at the Meetinghouse and in the winter in the Orange Congregational Church. For winter concerts, Dr. Heffernan assembles a twelve-plus-piece orchestra of professional musicians and soloists to augment the thirty-five-member chorus from towns throughout the Pioneer Valley and North Quabbin with several singers from Keene, New Hampshire.

QVPM cultivates a classical repertoire that has included opera, masses by great composers, twentieth-century music, art songs, and selections from light opera. Local composers Carolyn Brown Senier and Richard Chase of Orange and Allison Pollitt of Athol have debuted works with QVPM.

Frequent soloists have been John Salvi of Haverhill, baritone; Ethan Bremner of Norwood (formerly of Athol), tenor; Pollitt of Athol, mezzo and soprano; and Lynn Boudreau, soprano, and Candi Fetzer, mezzo, both of Orange.

The chorus rehearses weekly during autumn, winter, and spring in the Meetinghouse when the temperature permits and in the New Salem Congregational Church when it doesn't.

The opera concert was a slight departure for choristers. They had previously sung a few pieces from opera, but this concert presented a complete program of opera choruses, solos, and duets.

The QVPM singers were really energized by the concert. Hugh Field of New Salem, a relative newcomer to the chorus, was bursting with excitement after the concert. "This 'Afternoon at the Opera' concert was a wonderful mix of lovely pieces, which we sang beautifully in Italian, French, German, or English," he said. "Our conductor Charles Heffernan made inspired choices and then put the pieces in such a nice order. Many songs were cheery, and we wore colorful accessories to match, with the whole program a lot of fun."

Other local singers were just as excited. "What a great concert Sunday!" exclaimed Harry Haldt of Athol. "All our hard work really paid off. For opera lovers, it was a "best of"' highlights concert; for those new to opera, it was nine operas in one. And everyone recognizes at least one tune from *Carmen*."

Soloist Pollitt, who sang a long excerpt from *Carmen*, remarked, "What a lively concert it was! It was just plain fun. Never have I seen so many excited faces or heard so much applause from the audience. Everyone in the whole house was having a blast! Best of all, my nine-year-old, who probably knew the pieces by heart from hearing his mom practice since September, was gleaming with enthusiasm for opera!"

Chase was impressed not only with the sound but the total ambiance of the day. "I can't express how magnificent it was to be immersed in such sonic beauty," he said. "And did anyone notice how the sun filtered through the stained glass? What an afternoon!"

Some singers for the opera concert were from the Keene Chorale in New Hampshire, a chorus previously led by Heffernan. Betty Forrest was happy to join QVPM for the winter concert. "Those of us from the Keene Chorale who sing with you for the January concerts always enjoy our musical experience with QVPM and with Charles," she emailed from Keene. "You are a warm and welcoming group. The opera concert was tops!"

Quabbin Valley Pro Musica, resident chorus of New Salem's 1794 Meetinghouse, performs an annual concert in Central Congregational Church, Orange. Conductor Charles Heffernan provides an orchestra for a festive classical music event, above.

The rest of the performers couldn't contain their enthusiasm for the day:

"The concert was a hundred-dollar value," said William Howe Oldach of Athol. "I would have paid fifty dollars for Ethan and John's duet alone. And Allison and Candi were magnificent. Our friends who have attended most of our concerts loved it and said it was our best."

"On Sunday evening when I got home to my computer, I found myself emailing south Jersey and Philadelphia friends to rave about the QVPM and chamber orchestra concert in Orange," said Paul Shallers, a recent transplant from New Jersey to Greenfield. "Many people who live in the greater Philadelphia area, as I did until this past August, consider their city a mecca of good music, comparable in quality to New York's offerings. And most of those same people, including myself, would expect far less of a program of opera music presented in a small central Massachusetts town. Well, I am delighted to discover our preconceptions are simply wrong."

"I believe I inherited my love of music from my talented mom, Becky (Hunting) Gray who passed three years ago," said Jennifer Gray of New Salem, whose role in the concert included a dance during the *Eugene Onegin* sequence. "With her and Dad's encouragement I began singing at a young age and soon began dancing ballet at The Dance Studio in Orange. In high school at Mahar, I acted in musicals. I was excited last summer when our conductor proposed performing some opera in our next concert. My favorite selection was the waltz scene from *Onegin*. Since Dr. Heffernan wanted a couple to waltz during one of the interludes, I quickly volunteered! To combine all of my passions in one event made me very happy. I know Mom would have loved it if she could have seen it!"

"I felt the audience was very appreciative of the music we gave," said Ted Horman of Athol. "The audience was very active and generous with applause. As a performer in the group, sometimes I never know what the outcome of our rehearsals will bring, but the audience told us that the chorus, orchestra, and especially the soloists, performed especially well. I love to sing to a full house. It makes it all worthwhile.

"For me, the experience of singing in this concert was celestial," emailed John Nelson of Amherst. "The richness of choral music, glorious solo parts in Purcell, Verdi, Tchaikovsky, and Bizet, and emphasis, power (twenty-seven pieces!), and distinct coloration of the orchestra combined to create one of the happiest musical moments of my life. Singing in this chorus is a communal experience like none other—all of us listening, singing our individual parts, following and learning from our conductor, Charles Heffernan, and glorying in the genius and emotion of selections from some of the world's greatest composers. Truly, the whole is so much greater than the sum of its parts."

"It's a privilege for an amateur singer like me to be directed by a professional of the caliber of Dr. Heffernan," said Lisa McLoughlin of Northfield. "I always learn so much. This concert was especially memorable because of the professional orchestra and soloists. While singing with the chorus is always fun, the addition of these talented musicians made it a very special occasion."

"It was so wonderful to be part of this amazing song fest!!" said Judy Bisinger of Orange. "The soloists were beyond compare and the orchestra so splendid. I loved watching Charles direct this special production. He seemed to be thoroughly enjoying it. What a party! It was superb!"

"Participating in QVPM, making music with all of its members, is one of the greatest joys in my life," said Chuck Berube of Petersham. "Being a part of creating what we do together is something in which I feel great pride. I will greatly miss Monday nights these next three weeks."

"QVPM is a breath of fresh air and a surprising group of musicians," said Susan Marshall of Orange, another transplant to the area from New Jersey. "They offer a diverse and exciting repertoire of music, at once a thrilling and thoroughly delightful experience. The soloists enthralled the audience."

"I've sung with QVPM for more than thirty concerts," said Phil Rabinowitz of Royalston, "but this one was perhaps the most fun of any I've been involved in. As an opera lover, I've always wanted to sing some of the pieces we did. The glorious melodies, wonderful soloists (two of them drawn from QVPM itself), and pure joy and enthusiasm of the audience combined to make this a peak experience. My wife, sitting in the balcony, said she started grinning as soon as we began the first piece and never stopped until the concert ended. All in all, there's little better in life than singing beautiful music with friends. QVPM has been a delight for me from the beginning, and it just keeps getting better."

"Those of us in the chorus are ordinary people who come together simply because we love to sing," said Candace Anderson of Petersham. "The magic occurs through the gift of the music, interpreted through the genius of our conductor, Dr. Heffernan. We find ourselves sharing in something truly extraordinary. What a joy that is! Besides that, it's just plain fun!"

"My friends among the singers and my friends in the audience enjoyed themselves so much singing selections from the opera," said Senier. She summed up the performers' enthusiasm—"It was a glorious afternoon."

Ethan Stone, left, performs with Heidi-Jo Hanson and Jonathan Edwards at a 2006 Tool Town Live concert.

Bursting w/Music: Tool Town Live, Friendly Town Live

Ethan Stone

The music scene in the North Quabbin regions thrives—from the family-friendly free concerts in Athol and Orange and the great community orchestras in Orange and Petersham to performances in New Salem and the dozens of festivals that go on throughout the year.

The new year starts with Starry Starry Night, the free New Year's Eve spectacular in Orange featuring a plethora of music, comedy, art, and much more. It sprawls across numerous venues in downtown Orange.

Spring brings the Friendly Town Live concerts in Orange on Friday nights in May at Butterfield Park or in Orange Town Hall in case of rain. Friendly Town Live concerts are free for all ages and contain a wide variety of family-friendly musical styles such as rock, blues, jazz, Celtic, funk, folk, reggae, and much more.

The Orange Community Band takes over the bandstand at Butterfield Park on Friday nights beginning in June immediately after Friendly Town Live ends. The band features a veritable all-star lineup of some of the area's best talent performing songs you know and love in a fun concert band setting with brass, woodwinds, percussion, and more. Every Sunday night from the tail end of June to the beginning of August, the Petersham Brass Band entertains at The Common in Petersham. Now over a hundred years old, the Petersham Brass Band only gets better with time. The music—and the popcorn—are very tasty!

As if that wasn't enough, 1794 Meetinghouse in New Salem presents numerous reasonably priced concerts throughout June and July on Thursday and Saturday nights and Sunday afternoons in just about every possible musical style you can dream of. A combination of local talent, regional favorites, and nationally touring artists perform in an intimate, friendly atmosphere. Dorothy Johnson's well-known musical comedies, authored in the past with Andy Lichtenberg or Steven Schoenberg, brighten the Meetinghouse stage in alternate Septembers.

August and September bring the Tool Town Live concert series in Athol. Now in its twelfth year, the concert series electrifies the Uptown Common and Fish Park with classic rock and roll, blues, pop, classical, jazz, Celtic, funk, folk, reggae, and more on Saturday nights. Tool Town Live concerts are free for all ages, family friendly, and alcohol free. If inclement weather is in the forecast, Tool Town Live concerts are held in the Athol Town Hall, next to the most incredible library in the region, the newly improved Athol Public Library.

Now in its eighteenth year, the North Quabbin Garlic and Arts Festival in the fall at Forster's Farm in Orange has grown to become the heavyweight champion of arts and music in the region. From its humble beginnings of a handful of attendees to the epic spectacle that brings an enormous amount of positive energy to our North Quabbin region, the Garlic and Arts Festival includes ridiculous amounts of incredible food, art, dance, music, and did I mention *gaaaaaaaaahlic*!?!?

Also if you love music and art, don't miss the Celebrate the Harvest Festival; The Arts in Bloom Festival; Old Home Days in Warwick, Wendell, Petersham, and New Salem; winter open mic nights at the Royalston Town Hall and Athol Town Hall; Wendell's Full Moon Coffeehouse; Orange Word poetry readings—and don't forget *Midnight Madness* in Athol and Orange each December. Not only is midnight madness a great night to buy local, support local businesses, and be rewarded mightily for doing so with awesome discounts and deals, but it's also a great chance to see some of the area's best musical talent performing in multiple spots!

The list above doesn't even scratch the surface! These are just a very few of the wonderful venues, performers, and events in the North Quabbin area that I've had the lucky opportunity to be connected with in some way over the years! We as a community are also blessed to have one of the only truly independent radio stations left and still going strong, 97.3FM WJDF. The station supports hundreds of community events and contributes to the betterment of the region in many, many ways! Excitingly, WJDF is now hearable from anywhere in the world with an internet connection at www.wjdf.com. Wherever you may roam, WJDF will keep you up to date on the great things happening, musical and otherwise, in this wonderful North Quabbin region.

Making a Living by Performing Magic

Ed the Wizard

I am lucky. I like what I do, and I make a living at it. I started performing magic professionally in 1999; I went full time in 2006.

I grew up, perhaps like many other folks, having an interest in magic and knowing a few routines. I always enjoyed magic whether I was watching it on television, seeing a live stage show, or reading books about magic and magicians. I still marvel at others when I see a good performance. It makes no difference whether I know how the magic trick was done. If it is performed well, I am still amazed.

I love being with my audience and seeing faces light up with awe and hearing whispers of "How did he do that?"

Ed the Wizard engages children and adults with a magic performance during Montague's Mutton and Mead Festival.

Inspired by Harry Potter's Headmaster Albus Dumbledore, Ed the Wizard concocts his magic at his home in Orange.

Sometimes I laugh to myself as the most jaded of spectators suddenly starts to show interest when I perform my routines. Occasionally when I approach a group of folks and offer to perform my style of magic for them, most will say "yes," but one may say (and quite adamantly) "No!" As others in the group will still want to participate, I tell the one, "They would like to see something, and I will do this one effect for them, but you are not allowed to watch!"

Of course, that one does watch. Then before that person knows it, I have her! She now wants to see more.

Sometimes I take my audience from thinking that they know what I am about to do and how it is done to totally catching people unaware. Magic is all about having fun, making folks laugh, and having a good time.

I average over a hundred performances throughout the year. The summer months mean Summer Reading time at public libraries, and I perform for two and sometimes three different libraries each weekday with fairs on weekends. And I love it!

For public libraries, I adapt my program Reading Is Magic to fit the theme for that summer. For example, in 2014 the Massachusetts Summer Reading theme was "Fizz, Boom, Read!" I created Ed the Wizard's Alchemy Laboratory! My audiences not only helped me perform magic but learned how to perform effects using ordinary items from the kitchen. We defied gravity, peered through solid objects, and in a flash transformed water to ice.

Autumn is fair season. I have always enjoyed attending fairs, but now it is a part of my job to go. Fair season gives me the chance for up-close and personal magic with small-group audiences. These interactions last anywhere from a just few minutes with one or two effects to thirty to sixty minutes depending on the size and energy of a particular audience. I also make balloon animals for fair patrons and perform stage shows.

I spend fair season weekdays in my office making phone calls to libraries. Believe it or not, I start booking my library summer reading programs during the previous autumn's fair season.

During the winter, I perform for schools and libraries as well as holiday parties. At schools I offer several programs including Reading Is Magic, which emphasizes the importance of building reading skills and Math Is Magic, which demonstrates how I use math to perform mind-reading effects. I also teach a class in balloon-animal twisting and a workshop about magic for after school events.

Winter tends to be the slower part of my year, and I have time to research and practice new routines. I like to keep my performances exciting and fresh for my audiences whether it is their first time or the hundredth with me.

I also attend conventions during the winter. There, I meet with delegates from libraries, the Parent-Teacher Organization, fairs, and park and recreation departments. Conventions offer performers like me a chance to showcase our programs, meet face to face with the buyers, and take bookings. Scheduling events is a constant part of my job.

Living in the North Quabbin area has many advantages. Centrally located in New England, the North Quabbin is perfect for my work and travels. We have six crossroads leading out of Orange, and I can be anywhere in the Northeast with very little effort and often within two hours or less. My average drive is about one and a half hours—I listen to a lot of books on CD.

As outdoor enthusiasts, my family and I enjoy hiking in the Quabbin and along many other area trails. We also enjoy rock and ice climbing, white water rafting, canoeing, snow shoeing, and camping, all right here in the North Quabbin area. It is rural and out of the way, but not too far out of the way. It is a great place to live, have a family, and perform magic.

Honest Weight Artisan Beer

Sean Nolan and Jay Sullivan

BEERS

GOOD NAME GRISETTE

A pale, dry, sessionable beer brewed with locally grown and malted wheat, rye, and buckwheat, floral European hops, and our house Saison yeast.

OG - 11°P
FG - 1.7°P
ABV - 4.8%

BRANCH BRIDGE PALE ALE

Pale Malt, Vienna, and Oats provide a lush base for this juicy American Pale Ale. Liberally kettle hopped and dry-hopped twice with Centennial, Mosaic, Chinook, and Columbus.

OG - 12.5°P
FG - 2°P
ABV - 5.4%

THE TULLY

An American India Pale Ale brewed with Pale Malt, Vienna, Caramel Malt, Oats, and Dextrose. Huge hop character is developed with kettle additions of Magnum, Chinook, and Centennial, while two unique dry hop additions include Mosaic, Equinox, and Centennial.

OG - 16°P
FG - 2.5°P
ABV - 7%

Honest Weight Artisan Beer (HWAB) of Orange draws upon the rich history and strong community in the North Quabbin. Jay Sullivan and Sean Nolan, HWAB co-founders, brew, package, and distribute high-quality, small-batch beers that are associated strongly with the local communities of North Central Massachusetts and greater Massachusetts as a whole.

Owner Sean Nolan is a native of the North Quabbin region and a 2011 graduate of the brewing technology program at Chicago's Siebel Institute of Technology/World Brewing Academy. After completing his program, Sean went on to work as a brewer at the Cambridge Brewing Company, Idle Hands Craft Ales, and Enlightenment Ales—some of the New England area's most well-respected breweries. His co-owner Jay Sullivan was born in Lowell and is a graduate of the Salisbury, Vermont, American Brewers Guild's Intensive Brewing Science and Engineering program. He worked for the Cambridge Brewing Company for more than four years, starting as an Assistant Brewer and rising through the ranks to the position of head brewer. In that role, Jay led a team of brewers (including HWAB partner Sean Nolan) to achieve several medals at both the Great American Beer Festival and the World Beer Cup.

HWAB occupies industrial space for its brewery and tasting room at the Orange

Innovation Center in Orange. Visitors to HWAB will be able to enjoy the brewery's products in their onsite tasting room where customers can view the operation of the brewery while purchasing beer samples, beer by the glass, and beer to go in growlers.

HWAB will produce several beers year-round and, to start, exclusively on draft at area bars and the brewery tasting room. HWAB beers will include a rotating line-up of hop-forward American ales and rustic, Belgian-inspired Grisettes and Saisons. Bottled releases of unique-, wine-, or spirit-barrel-aged beers will be produced and available for retail sale, only in the HWAB tasting room. The beers represent styles known to be very sought after by beer aficionados. They require patience and skill to brew successfully.

HWAB focuses on creating a sustainable small brewing company, deeply rooted in the fabric of life in the North Quabbin, that will serve the desire for fresh, hand-crafted beer for discerning craft beer enthusiasts and neophytes alike. HWAB brewers want to make honest beer from quality, locally-sourced ingredients. The brewers aim to create a business that takes care of its employees, the community that supports it, and the environment around it. To that end, they will strive to use environmentally friendly products and practices, including reclaiming water for cleaning. HWAB will donate spent grain to local farms for animal feed and spent hops and yeast for compost.

HWAB represents the only brewery in the North Quabbin area and one of six breweries in Franklin County. The owners want to focus on creating craft beer in and for the area they love.

Quabbin Sky Vineyard Makes Wine from New Salem Grapes

Joyce Wiley

In the fall of 2004, Phil and I moved to New Salem, Massachusetts. We bought a lovely home in a beautiful location and were very excited about our new adventure. Our house came with two acres of land, one of them overgrown and needing to be mowed. Upon mowing the field, Phil discovered old grape vines growing on the ground—right on top. He staked them up, and we waited to learn if they were alive. They were, and we were on our way to becoming wine makers.

There were eight rows in all, and six came up one leaf at a time. That spring we learned our neighbor Fritz Von Mering had started the vines. He started the vineyard in the late sixties and seventies. He purchased the vines from the Rhine Valley, both French and German sides. "These are wine grapes," he told both Phil and me, "and I want you to make wine." We promptly replied that we did not know how to make wine or manage a vineyard. His reply was, "I know, but you can learn." And learn we did.

The University of Massachusetts Cold Springs Orchard and Vineyard in Belchertown is where we went for help. Phillip sent Sonia Schloemann an e-mail describing our situation. Sonia is a small fruit specialist with Northeast Sustainable Agriculture Research and Education at UMass. I will never forget the afternoon Sonia came to our house. Phil came running into the kitchen saying, "She came! She came."

"Who?" I replied.

"Sonia. Sonia Schloemann is here. Come out to meet her." That was the beginning of a nine-year friendship we have with Sonia, Shawn Burke, and everyone at Cold Springs. We went to them with every question beginners can have—and they were always there to answer. We would drop off bugs and leaves and anything that didn't look right to us on their desks. We would always get a reply and instructions on what to do next. You must understand how important this was to us. We knew nothing.

Sonia is a very busy person and travels throughout New England helping vineyards and fruit farms much larger than our vineyard. We only have one acre of vines and had even less at that time. She never left us out of the loop of information on seminars about both vineyard care and winemaking. We were introduced to other local winery

Finding themselves owners of a vineyard when they bought their home in New Salem from Fritz von Mehring, Phil and Joyce Wiley, above, learned to make wine.

owners. We made contact with Cornell University small-farm winery programs on canopy control and spraying techniques. Wayne Wilcox, Department of Plant Pathology at Cornell, has been a guiding light to us. Every year he puts out his report *Grape Disease Control*. We read every word, and I follow every suggestion he makes. We volunteered our time at Cold Springs during harvest, and Sonia paid us in kind with product. She said, "Now you must learn to make wine."

The first carboy (five gallons) of wine we ever made was our Aurore from the vines Fritz had planted. We harvested about seven gallons. What a treat. We had no equipment to speak of, so we crushed and de-stemmed by hand and created what winemakers call "must." All the work was done on our back step. We had a small hand press that worked fine. We collected the juice in a five-gallon fermentation bucket we had purchased with our winemaking 101 book. We did all the tests, added a quarter teaspoon of sulphur dioxide, and twenty-four hours later added wine yeast. Two days later, the must fermented in our kitchen.

The third day everything stopped. What a crisis. We made a quick phone call and learned the must needed heat; we had a stalled fermentation. We quickly brought the bucket outside to a beautiful eighty-five-degree day. Off it took to complete primary fermentation. It was time to put our wine (it was really wine then) in the carboy and add an airlock. We have learned to age our wine for a year. Then we bottle. We were so proud of that first seven gallons of wine and all that we had learned. Fritz died that summer before the grapes were harvested. He knew all the while of our progress and that there would be a harvest.

The real work started next with growing the vineyard out. We took cuttings from all the mother plants Fritz had planted and used them to propagate the vineyard. We now have 450 plants, and they consist of four varietals— Aurore, Totmur, and two yet to be determined. All the plants have to be DNA-tested to learn their correct identity before labeling. We purchase our red grapes from Cold Springs, as our vineyard has only white grapes. We work only with cold, hardy varietals developed for cold climates.

The plants are winter-hardy and more resistant to disease. They are hybrid plants. Aurore was developed in the 1860s in France. She and Totmur are the oldest. Corot Noir was released from Cornell University in 2006. We are truly a teeny vineyard of old vines and new wines at Quabbin Sky Vineyard.

In 2011 we became the first farmer winery in New Salem. We keep our winemaking process as natural to the grape as when we started. We do not use malolactic fermentation, and we do macerate the reds before and after fermentation. Our wines are cold-stabilized for balance. We do not fine or filter the wine before bottling. We age only in glass in stainless steel. All the work is done on premises. We name our wines after the towns incorporated into the Quabbin out of remembrance of the people who had to give up everything so this body of water could be formed. To date we make and sell eleven wines from our winery: reds–Frontenac, Chambourcin, Corot Noir, Noiret, Cabernet Franc and Vincent—and whites—Aurore, Chardonel, Cayuga, Vignole and LaCrosse.

Fritz told us, "I left you a little treasure. Now go and make wine."

photo courtesy of Bill Compton courtesy of
Athol Daily News

photo courtesy of Mike Castignaro courtesy of
Worcester Telegram and Gazette

*Jeff Baker and his father, Chuck, right foreground wearing visors, safely clear
the South Main Street bridge in Athol in 1979 and head for Orange, top,
during the annual River Rat Race. Near the start in 1982, canoeists jockey
for the lead.*

This Thing We Call the River Rat Race

Kathryn Chaisson with David W. Flint

Rhythmic pounding grows louder and faster as dozens of competing canoeists pumped with adrenaline thump the sides of their boats with their paddles. They anxiously and excitedly wait for the 1 pm boom of Pete Strong's cannon to signal the start of the annual nearly six-mile race down the Millers River. The starting point alongside Cass Meadow in Athol is narrow for the congestion of canoes. The Le Mans style fast start, where everyone goes at once, creates an aquatic traffic jam of rapid strokes and skilled maneuvering to avoid spills and collisions. Once racers pass under nearby South Main Street Bridge, the river widens. Supported by the cheers of onlookers, friends, and families perched along river banks from the beginning to the end at Hachey's Landing in Orange, the race for record time, trophies, and personal aspirations is on.

Since its inception in 1964, the Athol-to-Orange River Rat Race has grown into a weekend-long community and family-oriented event that includes a parade, pancake breakfast, the Big Cheese 5K road race, and Sunday Pro-Am and kayak races sponsored by local businesses and corporations. Annual volunteer work from many organizations and individuals contributes to a smoothly-running event. Annually occurring on the second Saturday and Sunday in April, race weekend attracts college students and others who have moved from the area to return to reunite with friends and family or participate in the race. The race brings curious visitors and paddlers from New England, throughout the United States, and other countries.

Orange natives Staff Sergeant Glen Rathburn and his wife Danielle Johnson Rathburn, stationed at Eielson Air Force Base in Alaska since 2013, returned to race in 2014. A former dedicated racer, Glen previously participated several times—three with his father and four with a school friend. 2014 marked his first race since 2004 and the second overall for Danielle, who paddled with her father Dan Johnson her first time. Glen has been in the military since June 2004, and the 2014 race was the first time schedules allowed the couple to be home for the race. "We couldn't pass up the chance to race in it. It is a blast to race and compete with people from all over the country," he said.

There is no discriminating when it comes to racers. Professional and recreational paddlers, race veterans, and bucket-list newcomers—locals and out-of-towners—compete together under various classes and canoe types. One year there were 410 registered canoes. Typically the number averages around 300.

For some it is a family affair. The children of paddlers Eliot and Beth Nottleson of Orange started canoing young: Marie, who in 2014 was thirteen, and Zachary, eleven, both first entered the race at eight years old. The Schlimmer siblings of Cortland, New York have won multiple trophies.

People of all ages have raced. Harry Wilcox of Connecticut entered the 2014 race at ninety-one with his daughter, Elizabeth Warder of Orange.

Some paddlers take the river challenge a little less seriously than others. On her registration form, one woman filled in the age blank with the word old.

Over the years, bystanders along the river have witnessed a variety of decorated canoes featuring favorite sports teams, mascots, and canoeists themselves dressed as pirates, moose, frogs, and giant rats. A group of spectators from their South Main Street vantage point watched as one team leisurely rode down the river while cooking on a small grill.

Local politicians, sportscasters, and journalists have participated in the race. Charlie Moore, a television celebrity known as the Mad Fisherman, rode in the lead boat one year. As he witnessed the race in progress, he proclaimed, "You call me crazy?"

In 2013, everyone celebrated the fiftieth anniversary of the Athol-to-Orange River Rat Race with a parade, fireworks, and a nostalgia race for a small group of race alumni competing for a case of beer. All six pairs of participants received the beer. The Batutis brothers, John Jr. and Mike, used the same aluminum canoe they used in the first official race in 1964.

The River Rat Race had humble beginnings that over decades evolved into a highly anticipated, widely attended early spring tradition. In 1962, a pair of local fishermen, Ed Gleba and Burl Pepperdine, wanted to fish in a deep, brush-filled spot on the river, so they purchased a three-hundred-dollar canoe from Piragis Boats near Brookside Road in Athol. The following spring as the ice broke, Ed suggested to Burl they take the afternoon off, drink a few beers, and

Sonny Soucie, left, and Art Forand of Athol won the first River Rat Race in 1964.

paddle down to Hachey's Landing after Burl's wife dropped them off at Cass Meadow with an agreed pickup time of four in the afternoon. The second year about the same time they did the same thing.

In 1964, Gleba and Pepperdine had a beer at the Silver Front Café in Athol, and Gleba told Pepperdine the river ice was breaking up. He suggested they take the next Friday afternoon off and "go down." Pepperdine agreed. Ken Young, sitting nearby, overheard the men and asked what they meant by "go down." Gleba explained "to town" by canoe, and Young said he'd like to join them along with friend Cliff Parcher. Sitting next to Young was Billy Gillis who said he'd go with Bill Blaser. About a half an hour later, Ted Crumb arrived and said he'd go down with Merritt Cleveland. Young suggested pooling two dollars per person or four dollars a canoe with four canoes, winner would get the money, and everybody would go down to Hachey's Landing "to drink it (the winners' money) up."

Barney Cummings, managing editor of the *Athol Daily News*, appeared in the Silver Front, heard the group talking about the ride down the river, and placed a blurb in the paper for the little canoe race. "Well,

Canoeists paddle downstream just below the South Main Street, Athol,
bridge in the tenth annual River Rat Race, 1973.

then they kept on getting more and more," Gleba recalled. Crumb and
Gleba decided to make a wooden plaque with label-maker-tape names
of entrants and others who helped out with the first race. There were
only eight signed up when the plaque was made, but there ended up
being twelve canoes for what Barney proclaimed the First River Rat
Spectacular, or the first official River Rat Race, March 21, 1964.

Sonny Soucie and Art Forand won the first race. Years later after
Sonny's death, the Soucie family decided to give a special award for
most canoes passed by a single pair of paddlers. Many consider the
Sonny Soucie/Art Forand Memorial Award the most prestigious prize
of the race.

For the first three race years, according to Gleba, Cecil Young
hollered, "Go!" because the canoes were close together. By the fourth
year, with fifty canoes spread out, Billy Gillis used a shotgun to signal
the start of the race. By 1968, the number of canoes rose to a hundred.

For years, Ted Crumb, above, served as River Rat Race maestro.

Pete Strong took over with his small cannon, and he started the race every year through 2014. In 2015, he passed the torch to his son Kris who lit the cannon for a new generation.

By the third year, the official race had become a major undertaking. River Rat Spectacular, Inc., spearheaded by Ted Crumb with help from individuals within the community, organized the annual event. In 1990, the *Athol Daily News* announced that the original crew of the River Rat Spectacular no longer wanted to run it. David Flint saw the article and suggested at a Chamber of Commerce meeting that the Athol Lions Club might be interested in taking over. The Lions board of directors accepted the responsibility of organizing the race. Flint brought Tom Lozier and Lyle Smith on board to do the work of coordinating the race.

Meanwhile, David Caldwell, owner of the Traverse Street Inn, started a fundraising effort with a prize of two benefit hockey games featuring retired Boston Bruins players. He told Flint he would step back and let the Lions oversee the River Rat Race so that the race carried on. Flint spent some time talking with Crumb at the Traverse Street bar and between drinks was able to convince the reluctant Crumb to hold the hands of the Lions for the first year. Crumb agreed as long as the Lions kept the Le Mans type start, the maximum eighteen-foot-canoe rule, and dropped the title Spectacular. In 1993, the Lions created the Ted Crumb Big Cheese Award to recognize a business or individual who has for many years contributed hard work to make the River Rat Race what it is today.

Gleba said he told Pepperdine, "You know, I never thought it would last this long. Never. If it wasn't for Ted Crumb, we wouldn't have done it."

It has been said that you cannot truly call yourself a local unless you have participated in the River Rat Race.

Libraries of the North Quabbin

Paula J. Botch

Many of my childhood memories are shrouded, just beyond my grasp, and I have no recollection of any particular libraries in Virginia or Maryland where I grew up. I do remember my mother's irritation when she found out that my schoolteachers gave assignments that required not one or two but at least three references. My parents had purchased a *World Book Encyclopedia* set so there would be plenty of information on hand at home for school projects, and they were pretty disappointed at having to continue to cart me and several younger siblings to a library anyway.

Libraries were and are quiet places, a refuge from the hubbub of everyday life. These days, they don't seem to maintain the rigid silence of years gone by, but they remain a welcoming retreat for me, places to browse and relax. No longer are libraries simply filled with books and periodicals, but DVDs and personal computers are available too. Meeting rooms are open for community use, and local artists display their talent in library galleries.

As an avid lifelong reader, I have filled my house with books—I can't seem to keep myself from buying or borrowing more. Whenever I find a book at a yard or library sale with a pocket still holding an old library card, crooked dates stamped in colorful ink, I am filled with incredible nostalgia.

When asked to do a project on libraries of the North Quabbin towns, I felt a bit of apprehension mixed with curiosity. Take photographs of the towns' libraries? And write about them too?

What was surprising and most disappointing in pursuing the North Quabbin libraries is how little information is readily available about them. Town libraries are extensions of their town governments, attached to town government websites, which are fairly bland and lack much in the way of historical information. The websites are somewhat symbolic of our times, like the conformity of big box stores or cemeteries that have uniform markers with bare-bones (pun intended) information about their subjects in the ground below. The reality is that most of the libraries are small with small budgets and staffs. Working on their websites is low priority against their many other tasks. Given that hurdle, I found true pleasure visiting libraries where online information was sparse to non-existent. The librarians were friendly and helpful, and I am so grateful for their assistance.

Although some websites don't have much to say about their town libraries, the buildings are unique. Most of them are quaint structures, small and white, that reflect our early American and New England rural roots. Others are quite grand— the beautiful storybook-like stone Petersham Memorial Library is one— and Athol Public Library is a Carnegie library.

Athol—Athol Public Library

photo by Paula J. Botch

Athol Public Library

Library service in Athol dates back to 1830, and in 1878, the Athol Library Association was formed. It is to this early group the Athol Public Library is directly related. The library was first located in the second story of the School Street home of Joel M. Doane and then moved to his barn. Later, the library was moved to the Academy of Music building on Exchange Street.

In 1914, Laroy S. Starrett leased land to build a new library, and Wilson H. Lee of New Haven opened negotiations (for the second time) with the Carnegie Corporation to fund a new library building. Two years later, the town of Athol accepted a grant of twenty-two thousand dollars. The new library, turned over to the town in August 1918, was designed by W.H. & Henry McLean of Boston and built in a simplified Classical Revival style by Fellows and Ducworth Co., Inc. of Brookline,

Massachusetts. The library was the first building in town to have air conditioning, added in 1969.

In October 2012, a groundbreaking ceremony took place to renovate and expand the library, a huge modern addition off the back of the original building. The newly expanded Athol Public Library was dedicated on January 25, 2014.

Erving—Erving Public Library

Erving Public Library

In 1882, the town of Erving's citizens voted to accept books from the Library Association and to establish the main library at Erving Center with a branch at Millers Falls. The books were to be divided equally between the two locations, although no provision was made for a public place to keep the books. Two men were paid a few dollars for librarian services and room rent.

In 1885, Mrs. Sarah Holton Ballou, a former resident then living in Detroit, Michigan, offered the town a gift of 250 volumes of current and classic literature on the condition the town establish and maintain a free public library. Although published town history barely mentions James Moore (1820-1869), he was a landholder, industrialist, and farmer. His land was donated for a library, school, and park.

These days, a small white-sided Cape style building houses the Erving Public Library. It was built in 1961 and holds roughly nine thousand items. The Erving Public Libraries (Center Library and

Erving Library at Millers Falls) merged in 2003 to become the Erving Public Library.

New Salem—New Salem Public Library

photo by Paula J. Botch

New Salem Public Library

New Salem Public Library is tied with the town of Greenwich, one of those sadly lost to the Quabbin Reservoir. Greenwich established its public library 1891 with a donation of two hundred dollars from the estate of Stephen P. Bailey followed by a number of donations from other trust funds and estates, all instrumental to New Salem's library.

New Salem's library opened in March 1890 in the old town hall where it remained for twenty-three years. In 1894, a gift of five hundred dollars was made by Pamela Butterfield for the purchase of nonfiction books. In 1913, the library moved to a large room in New Salem Academy for an annual rent of forty-five dollars.

As the date approached for flooding of the town of Greenwich, the townspeople voted to give their library books, furniture, and library trust funds to the town of New Salem. The vote took place at a Greenwich town meeting, likely in 1938. The town of Greenwich provided 3,500 books.

In 1968, New Salem Academy closed, and by 1970 the library moved back to its original site in the old town hall. Renovations were done over a four-year period. In 1973, Friends of Library formed and is still in existence today. The library is located in an old schoolhouse, a small white clapboard structure built in 1839 and recently renovated and rededicated.

North Orange—Moore-Leland Library

photo by Paula J. Botch

Moore-Leland Library, North Orange

In the winter of 1894-95, Asula P. Goddard made a bequest of three thousand dollars to purchase books to be housed in a permanent location in North Orange. Prior to that, books were ferried back and forth from the main library in Orange at the expense of the town. By 1883, a large collection was in the home of R.O. White.

There was much discussion as to the advisability of accepting Mrs. Goddard's bequest. Through the efforts of several interested people in town, the legacy was voted on and accepted at the annual town meeting in March 1895. Plans started immediately for North Orange Branch Library.

Several houses were considered as a location to keep the library collection, but the trustees decided that a large room in the old Perry house (Old Perry Tavern) was most suitable. Equipment, tables, and shelves were brought in and set up. In October of 1895, Orange

212

librarian Mrs. Pomeroy and her husband brought many boxes of books and helped set up for the new branch's opening day. Later, another room was added to the library as the collection grew larger. Today, Moore-Leland Library houses approximately seven-thousand volumes.

Orange—Wheeler Memorial Library

photo by Paula J. Botch

Wheeler Memorial Library, Orange

The Orange Free Public Library was one of the first established in America and opened in 1859 with 286 volumes, although the town's library history may date back to the 1830s. A room in the town hall housed the library for many years, but it became increasingly difficult to work quietly there. In 1912, there was talk of remodeling the town hall with prospects of a real memorial building.

The library moved to Washburn's Block at East Main and Water streets and construction on Wheeler Memorial Library began in 1912. The library is sixty by sixty-eight feet, of mottled gray faced brick with Indiana limestone, underpinning and steps of Fitchburg granite, roof of green slate, and enough space to hold eighteen thousand volumes. The library also originally housed the Orange Historical and Antiquarian Society.

Wheeler Memorial Library, dedicated in 1914, is at the corner of East Main and Grove streets and built on the site of the former home of Dr.

I. T. Johnson. It was given to the town by Alvira Wheeler Thompson in memory of her late husband, John W. Wheeler, who was president and treasurer of the New Home Sewing Machine Company.

The trustees' report at the end of 1914 states "Our new library is an ornament to the town . . ."

Petersham—Petersham Memorial Library

Petersham Memorial Library

The public library in the town of Petersham began in 1879. The historic fieldstone building that houses the beautiful Petersham Memorial Library was built in 1890, and its architect was Edmund Wilson. Located on the town common, it is one of the more prominent buildings in the area. In addition to maintaining the library's collection, the town demonstrates a strong commitment to preserve the architectural integrity of the building and memorials within the building.

The library provides the community with a diverse and rich collection that nurtures a love of books and reading and fosters the communication of ideas and information. The library is also home to a special collection of materials of local and regional history and genealogy.

Phillips Free Public Library, Phillipston

In 1800, a town meeting was called to form a library society in Phillipston, and books for lending were likely kept in the home of designated librarian Rev. Ezekial Bascom. The town's library was established in 1860 with a gift of five thousand dollars from Jonathan Phillips of Boston, nephew of Lieutenant Governor Phillips for whom the town is named. Jonathan saw that Phillipston took a special interest in the cause of education and ranked very high in its support of schools, motivating him to provide the money for a library.

Phillips Free Public Library opened in 1862 in Gould's Tavern on the common along the stagecoach route from Athol to Templeton. The town furnished the room and librarian and the Phillips Fund bought the books. In 1868, the library moved to the home of librarian Tina Chaffin on Baldwinville Road where it remained until 1891. The library moved to a room designed for the library in the town hall and had a collection of eight thousand books. In 1911, the library deposited 100 books in each district school to make books more accessible to people living in outlying areas. Teachers at the schoolhouses kept the records.

In 1952, the library moved to its current home, Number 1 Schoolhouse, a little white clapboard building just off the town common. The schoolhouse was built and opened in 1790 and closed in 1948. The side door used by library patrons today was not there when the building was a school, only a front door that is no longer in use. Friends of the Library continue to help upgrade the building through fundraising and grants providing such items as curtains, windows, and an addition for a children's room.

Royalston—Phinehas S. Newton Library

Phinehas S. Newton Library, Royalston

Royalston is likely one of the earliest towns in Worcester County to have a library. A "social library" had been established in the town in 1778, only thirteen years after the town's incorporation. The Library Company of Royalston later became the Social Library of Royalston that lasted for seventy-one years and was dissolved in 1849.

The Public Library of Royalston has its roots in the Ladies' Benevolent Society established in 1824. The members of the society recognized early on the need for a public library and, in January 1874, they began fundraising activities. The library opened in October 1874 with 434 volumes and remained in the care of the society until the town formally accepted it in 1880.

Phinehas S. Newton was a native and lifelong resident of Royalston. He was a member of a committee called Overseers of the Poor. At the March 1910 town meeting, Mr. Newton announced that he would donate ten thousand dollars for building a new library provided the town procured a suitable site. Land on the town common owned by William H. Hill of Brookline was chosen as a potential site, and Mr. Hill donated the land in memory of his wife. Work began on the library in August 1910. This lovely library of red brick with brown sandstone trimmings was dedicated in June 1911. Its Victorian architecture mirrors past grandeur of the town's common, a true gem for the community.

Warwick—Warwick Free Public Library

photo by Paula J. Botch

Warwick Free Public Library

In 1815, a first step was taken toward providing a library for Warwick townspeople by the women of the town under the guidance of Reverend Preserved Smith. Meetings were held at the center schoolhouse and members paid twenty-five cents annually toward the purchase of books. The association continued until 1842 when it was voted to unite with the Social Library formed two years prior. The Society for the Promotion of Peace and Useful Knowledge, expanded by a Lyceum, was dissolved in 1840 and it was proposed to create the Warwick Social Library.

William Cobb, who served as librarian and treasurer in the preceding societies, continued in the same capacities, and the library

217

was kept in his store. After Cobb's death in 1853, Quartus M. Morgan was chosen as librarian by the trustees, and the books were moved to his home. He served until 1869, when the Lyceum, reorganized in 1855, decided to rejuvenate the library, and the Warwick Library Association was formed.

In November 1870, the town of Warwick voted to appropriate a hundred dollars for the purpose of a public library. In March 1871, the town voted to accept the proprietors' library.

The library was located in several places over the years but finally found its permanent home in the town's former Baptist church. Membership of the church had dwindled to the point that services were discontinued, and the church was offered to the town for a library building. The town gratefully accepted, funds were provided to make the necessary alterations to the building, and it was ready for occupancy in 1919. Electricity was installed in 1929. Renovations were done in 1999 and 2000, and an addition to the library was made in 2000. Warwick Free Public Library is a lovely white building that graces the town's common.

Wendell—Wendell Free Library

photo by Paula J. Botch

Wendell Free Library

Wendell's Library Society was formed in 1821, and a library was housed in one room of the town hall until the Wendell Town Library was built in 1921. Still in existence, the tiny building is Colonial Revival style and the only twentieth century building in the historic center.

In 2006, plans were made to renovate the 170-year-old town office building and the library was going to move to larger quarters there. The building served as Wendell's town hall from 1846 until the early twentieth century, was later used as a school, and then housed town offices since 1990. In July 2006, a tornado struck Wendell, badly damaging that building, and it was torn down in August 2006. Soon after, the decision was made to build a replica of the old town office, based on design plans by architect Margo Jones already in place for the renovation.

In July 2008, Wendell Free Library celebrated the first anniversary of opening the new building. Groups from across the state and region found the new library "the place to see." Featured in the publication *Library Journal* in its annual review of "The Year in Architecture," the library was among twenty-four of two hundred American libraries singled out for special mention in an article called "Library Buildings 2007: Going, Going, Green."

On the signs in the photo: "STOP FUELING THE WAR MACHINE", "ESTIMATED IRAQI DEAD 654,000", "3017 DEAD ? HOW ? MANY ? MORE ? ?", "NO SURGE IN IRAQ", "PEACE"

When the United States contemplated invading Afghanistan in 2001 after 9/11, some in the North Quabbin began an eight-year weekly Saturday silent vigil for peace in Memorial Park, Orange near the Peace Statue. Numbering as many as forty or as few as two, men and women stood with North Quabbin Women in Black through 2009. With the US bombing of sites in Syria, Afghanistan, and Iraq in 2014, Women in Black resumed the vigil on the third Wednesday of each month.

photo from www.mass.gov
Quabbin Reservoir Fishing Guides

Quabbin Reservoir flooded four central Massachusetts towns and parts of others in the 1930s to provide drinking water for metropolitan Boston. The displaced, their descendants, and many residents of the North Quabbin see the Quabbin as a symbol of urban indifference to rural concerns. An ironic consequence of Quabbin Reservoir involves its beautiful nature preserve, attractive to hikers and anglers.

North Quabbin Shadows

Phil Zahodiakin

Long before they turned it into One Big Water,
the valley was known as the Quabbin:
an Algonquin word meaning
"place of many waters."
Its indigenous inhabitants were loosely-knit families
known as the Nipmuck: an Algonquin word
meaning "fresh water people."
Who knows what they thought and felt
while watching European settlers
harnessing their riverine heritage with water wheels,
which, like the "water people,"
are mostly forgotten—especially out east—where
very few people seem to know the source of their water.
Could it be the Charles?
Hopefully not, rowers might smirk.
And if they're informed that their water comes from
one of America's largest purpose-built reservoirs,
they're likely to shrug indifferently,
which is an interesting contrast
to the attitude in New York City,
where most residents seem to know that their water
comes from an upstate reservoir whose watershed,
they will tell you, must be protected from
environmental insults such as fracking and pipelines.
But, where is the gratitude for the Quabbin?
Why aren't the politicians writing bills that would help
rebuild the mill towns rusting along the rivers
where the "water people" once fished and trapped?
They're willing to spend a billion dollars to rebuild
a rail line from Boston to a decaying city which,
despite the interstate highways in its midst,
has failed to recapture much of its former glory.

Do the politicians really believe that
commuter rail service will spark a renaissance in a city
where major highways, a nearby port,
and an ocean of commercial space
barely budge investors' eyebrows?
Meanwhile, as North Quabbin commuters drive
along a ribbon of two-lane blacktop,
many of them may be wondering why the politicians
haven't proposed to study, much less rebuild,
the old rail line linking the North Quabbin to the east.
Is Beacon Hill really oblivious to the shadows
falling across the Quabbin watershed?
Shadows cast by smokestacks rising
from empty mills and factories;
shadows cast by all those retired
workers lining up at food pantries;
shadows cast by streetlights that might
stay dark when the sun goes down;
shadows cast as warnings of a greedy, methane pipeline
that doesn't seem to promise any fuel or jobs
in return for scarring the lands of the "fresh water people."
To be sure, the North Quabbin still casts
many lovely shadows from the oak trees,
maples, birches, and evergreens
in its dense forests,
where hikers and residents stroll,
writers find seclusion, and
fairies play hide-and-seek in the ferns.
But the strangest shadows are as hard to see as the fairies,
for they only occur if a little sunlight trickles through
the murky currents descending into empty foundations
that once held stores and schools and homes in the towns
that were flattened and submerged for a reservoir that displaced
those inhabitants as coldly as their ancestors had made refugees
of the "water people."

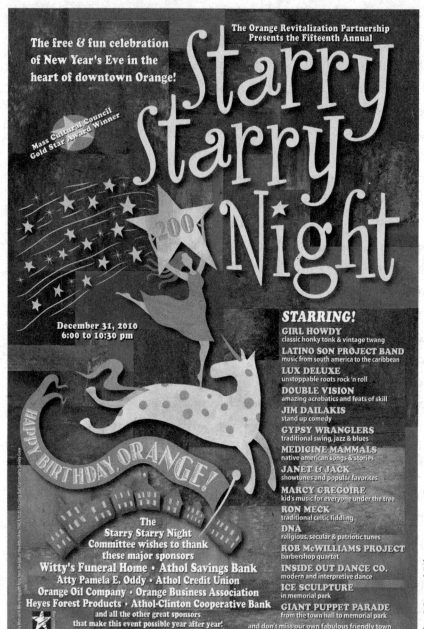

poster by Manuel King

Starry Starry Night is the free and fun celebration of New Year's Eve held annually in the heart of downtown Orange. Since 1996, the festival has brought music, magic, comedy, storytelling, dance, giant puppets, ice sculpture, and fireworks to the people of the North Quabbin. In 2006, the event was awarded the Massachusetts Cultural Council's Gold Star Award for Excellence in Arts Programming.

The Orange Revitalization Partnership
Presents the Sixteenth Annual

Starry Starry Night

December 31, 2011
6:00 to 10:30 pm

The free & fun celebration
of New Year's Eve in the
heart of downtown Orange!

In memory
of Wes Blackmer

ROBIN FOX
stand up comedian

GREEN RIVER STRING BAND
country, bluegrass & old time fiddle tunes

MELANIE & THE BLUE SHOTS
classic rhythm & blues

GROOVE SHOES
groove-oriented funk

LUI COLLINS
family-friendly folksinger & songwriter

THOUSAND ACRE JAZZ BAND
traditional jazz, swing & blues

EDDIE RAYMOND
comedy & magic

AMANDLA CHORUS
songs of justice, freedom & peace

RICHARD CHASE
singer/songwriter

NICOLE WANDER
puppet theater

INSIDE OUT DANCE CO.
ballet, jazz, tap & modern dance

ICE SCULPTURE
by Mark Bosworth and Tom Kellner

GIANT PUPPET PARADE
from the town hall to memorial park

and don't miss our own fabulous friendly town

FIREWORKS FINALE!
starrystarrynightorange.blogspot.com

MCC   massculturalcouncil.org

Poster design by Manuel & Mary King

The Starry Starry Night Committee
wishes to thank these major sponsors:
Witty's Funeral Home • Athol Savings Bank • TD Bank
Atty Pamela E. Oddy • Orange Oil Company • Orange Business Association
Workers' Credit Union • Bank of America • Athol Credit Union

poster by Manuel King

poster by Manuel King

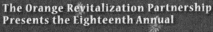

poster by Manuel King

poster by Manuel King

Bios of Contributors *to* Uniquely North Quabbin

Earle Baldwin is an Athol native. He chose to return from healthcare work in the Middle East to the cohesive community of the greater Millers River Watershed area. Serving on town committees influences his political positions. Long association with natural surroundings forged commitment to preservation of our fragile safe water supply. The solid, loyal, and non-intrusive residents of this community are a great comfort to him. Perhaps his comment, "Here, I am home" says all one needs to know about him.

Karl and Doris Bittenbender were high school sweethearts in Arlington, Virginia where they lived just a few miles apart. From there Karl went on to the University of Idaho and the US Navy, while Doris finished college at Wittenberg University in Ohio. They were married shortly after her graduation and settled in Charleston, South Carolina, until Karl finished his Navy obligation. From there to Chicago where Karl enrolled in seminary and Doris was a parish worker; then on to Orange, where Karl served as minister of Bethany Lutheran Church for six years. He moved on from that to jobs in rural housing, UMass Extension, MassSave, North Quabbin Chamber of Commerce, Shawmut Bank, and a business consulting company in Holyoke. Meanwhile, Doris served as town accountant for Orange for twenty years. Some of Karl's jobs involved a commute because they had both fallen in love with the Orange area so decided to buy a house and stay put while raising their two children while also raising sheep. Now, forty years later, they are still here . . . and still enjoying the area and lifestyle it provides. They are happy to be living where they can reach either the ocean or the mountains in two hours or less. They also enjoy volunteer opportunities and, of course, house and barn projects.

Johnny M. Botch, born in Washington, DC, moved frequently as part of a military family. He spent half of his childhood in Germany where he saw the ruins of World War II in the process of being rebuilt. He took pictures of the sights as the family traveled all over the country. Years later, he joined the Navy and enjoyed visiting many parts of the world, again using his camera along the way, not knowing if or when he would see those places again. Realizing how fleeting life and images are, he considers his photos "moments in time." Johnny resides in Orange, with his wife Paula and two cats. He is a dedicated military veteran and member of the American Legion. He pursues photography as a hobby and an art. His favorite subjects are flowers and natural landscapes.

Paula J. Botch is a writer and photographer who embraces the arts and creativity. She enjoys working in community theater and often participates in spoken word events. Her poetry is free verse, described by some as little stories that provide glimpses into moments and events. Paula's photography evolved from a casual activity to become a conscious artistic endeavor. She sees amazing images almost everywhere and captures nature's beauty as well as documenting old and forgotten places. She loves whimsy and finding the extraordinary in the ordinary. Born in Key West, Florida and oldest of five children, Paula grew up in Illinois, Virginia, and Maryland. Her parents, Massachusetts natives, returned after her father's Navy retirement, and Paula relocated from Maryland shortly after. She resides in Orange where she lives with her husband Johnny and two cats.

Mara Bright is a freelance writer and writing workshop leader in rural Massachusetts. Nurturing her connection with the land has always been an essential element in her life. She is an avid gardener, hiker, kayaker, and cross country skier. She also practices and teaches Breema bodywork and its underlying spiritual message. As an astrologer and intuitive reader, she sees clients.

Photographer **David Brothers** worked at prepress in the offset printing industry for more than thirty years. He began taking photos in the late 1990s when he bought a digital camera for a friend who did not use it. The friend suggested David use the camera, and David discovered that, on vacations, he became obsessed with the viewfinder. Soon, he was taking photos for publication.

Jon Chaisson was born and lived in Athol for most of his life. He lives in San Francisco with his wife Amanda, way too many books, and a ridiculously large music collection. He writes about music at his blog *Walk in Silence* (jonchaisson.com) and the writing life at *Welcome to Bridgetown* (welcometobridgetown.com).

Athol native **Kathryn Chaisson** has been a spectator of the Athol-Orange River Rat Race for many years and covered it as a reporter for the *Gardner News* in the 1980s. In 2013 she joined the Athol Lions Club and has served on the River Rat Planning Committee and participated in the canoe race judging. She took her first ever canoe ride down the Millers River in 2013 with Dianna (Flint) Dugas, a veteran River

Rat Race participant and women's class trophy winner. Chaisson is the author of Athol's Historic Buildings & Places and local tourism brochures. She has worked as a newspaper reporter, freelance writer, editor, proofreader, and historic researcher. She received her BA in media at Worcester State College and has been writing since childhood. She is a member of The Barnestormers, a local writer's group and is an advertising representative for the *Athol Daily News*.

Kathy Chencharik lives in North Central Massachusetts with her husband, dog, and cat. She is a free-lance writer whose poetry, fiction, articles, and letters have appeared in the *Athol Daily News, Gardner News, Greenfield Recorder, Fitchburg Sentinel,* and *Worcester Telegram* newspapers and *Birds & Blooms, Worcester,* and *Green Living* magazines. She earned honorable mention in *Alfred Hitchcock Mystery Magazine's* "The Story That Won" numerous times. *A Patchwork Christmas* (Haley's 2000) included her first published short story "S.A.N.T.A" and poem "Rights Before Christmas." Her short story "Shot By Mistake" was published in *Deadfall* (a Level Best Books anthology, 2008) for which she also won the cover photography contest. In 2011 she won the Derringer Award for best flash fiction for "The Book Signing" in *Thin Ice* (a Level Best Books anthology, 2010).

Robert Collén was born in Orange. He lived there most of his life with his wife Gloria and family. A graduate of Clark University, he served in the United States Air Force during the Korean War. He was the human resource executive at Rodney Hunt Company in Orange for more than thirty-eight years. He and his wife were touring motorcyclists and put on some two hundred thousand miles in their travels throughout the United States and Canada. He published three collections of his poems: *A Few Pianos,* Lynx House Press (1978); *Burning World,* Haley's (1997); and *Sailing in the Blue,* ByLine Press (2004). When he died in 2014, he was working on another collection of poems, tentatively titled *Notes on the Sublime.*

Carol Courville is the original and only executive director at Athol-Orange Community Television (AOTV). She received her BS from Newhouse School of Communications, Syracuse University, Syracuse, New York. She worked for ten years at Greater Media Cable, Worcester. While there, she honed her video production skills as a production assistant and public access director. At AOTV, she has trained more than six hundred residents to create their own TV programs and is constructing a noncommercial radio station WVAO-

LP, 105.9 for the community. Carol has devoted her energy to the North Quabbin area as treasurer of the Athol-Orange Area Rotary Club and a board member of North Quabbin Chamber of Commerce. She resides in Fitchburg with her husband Jim Brigley and son Lucas. She also enjoys time with her daughter Jessica and two grandchildren. Like many New Englanders, she is an avid Red Sox and Patriots fan.

Cynthia Crosson-Harrington moved to Petersham from California and put down permanent roots. She taught for many years in the behavioral science department at Fitchburg State University until 2002. Cynthia divides her time between work as a minister at First Congregational Church, Whately, and as a writer. Her books are mostly in the field of child welfare, including *Understanding Child Abuse and Neglect*. She is at work on a college text for those who will work with veterans and their families. Cynthia developed and helps administer the Trauma Assistance Dog Program of NEADS/Dogs for Deaf and Disabled Americans in Princeton. Her book *Only Daddy's Dog* (Haley's) explains to children the purpose of a service dog. She plans two more children's books about service dogs. The joy of her life is her own service dog Dandi Lyon, who is helping her with a memoir about her work with service dogs.

Candace R. Curran not only writes poetry, she champions it. She is the only adult poet twice named western Massachusetts Poet's Seat laureate. She is founder of Interface, a collaboration of word and image, a unique North of Quabbin exhibition of original visual art and poetry created and presented by participants in pairs or more. Since 1992, Interface has migrated around the area and involved more than a hundred visual artists and poets in more than ten distinct presentations. Curran is a frequent featured reader at poetry events. She has orchestrated several workshops for new and seasoned poets of all ages. Her poetry appears in chapbooks and the book Bone Cages, all published by Haley's of Athol, Massachusetts. Her poems are also found in periodicals, anthologies, and on the occasional Volvo hood. Follow her work and appearances at http://candacecurran.blogspot.com/.

Lynn Dudley's love of quilting started when she was very young, probably as she lay snuggled under a handmade, well-used quilt while visiting her great grandparents. The colors, patterns, stitching, warmth, and coziness delighted her. She never thought about making a quilt until a gift of a wedding quilt for her younger sister seemed just the thing. She found books on quilting and got started. As she worked on one quilt, ideas for other quilts jumped to mind, and she realized she was bitten by the quilting bug. She has been quilting since 1983. She has made quilts for family and friends' birthdays and weddings, for 1794 Meetinghouse and church raffles, and for the Orange Congregational Church centennial. She has worked as an RN for forty-three years and loves it. In retirement, she will spend her time gardening, reading, and quilting.

Ami Fagin is a New Salem-based visual artist specializing in the traditional art form of manuscript illumination, including ketubot, Jewish wedding documents. She is author of *Beyond Genocide*, an emerging series of illuminations narrating visual perspective on global incidents of genocide and mass violence. An independent scholar in genocide studies, she conducts research/seminars, lectures, workshops, and advisory work on global initiatives of memory and memorialization. She has contributed to the African Union Human Rights Memorial Project in Addis Ababa, Ethiopia and the Fifth International Symposium on Genocide and the Pursuit of Justice in Dhaka, Bangladesh. Ami served on the advisory board of the International Association of Genocide Scholars and regularly publishes editorials, reviews, and essays on genocide, art, and twenty-first-century expression and education. Her work represents a meta-modernist approach to materials, techniques, and theoretical principals used in manuscript illumination as a re-mediated visual art form for contemporary consideration.

Surrounded by woods and fields, **Susie Feldman** lives atop a hill in Athol. She spends much of her time in forest care, creating a trail system for walking and horseback riding. She enjoys taking her horses and donkeys through the woodlands. Managing the land and sharing its beauty with others are two of her interests. A retired educator, she loved teaching art in the Orange and Athol elementary schools. She feels that having been able to encourage creativity and originality in youngsters was an immensely satisfying way to spend her working years. Her paternal family has resided in Athol for the previous three generations. She is married to Ben Feldman, longtime Athol Town Treasurer. All the Feldmans' children and grandchildren live in the Athol area. Susie believes the sense of community resulting from growing up in a rural town such as Athol strengthens and enriches the lives of its people.

Hugh Field knows New Salem's geography pretty well by now, having been an assessor for three years and then a US census worker. He felt that it was the quickest way to get to know local people—and he found them delightful. He now is chair of the planning board and a member of the broadband committee, Friends of Historic New Salem, and Quabbin Valley Pro Musica. Previously he lived with his wife Sharon in Shirley, and for thirty years before that, in Norwood, having spent his teen years in Boston. Born in Manhattan, he spent most of his childhood in London but has stuck to Massachusetts ever since. His two teenage weeks at Audubon's Wildwood Nature Camp in Barre brought him back to the Quabbin. Having finally reached "the middle of nowhere," he is happy. Retired from state employment, Hugh has two grown children and two lovely granddaughters.

Rick Flematti is a lifelong resident of the North Quabbin region. Retired from the construction industry, he has turned his love of nature and photography into a full time passion. He began in the photographic film days documenting his fly-fishing trips and soon found he spent as much time taking photographs as he did fishing (much to the relief of the fish). Rick says that photographing in your home territory has big advantages: familiarity for one and the ability to return repeatedly when the light and seasons change. "I hope to inspire an appreciation of our natural habitat and the living things that depend upon it." He is found frequently hiking and biking with his camera searching for his next image of the North Quabbin woods. Rick resides in Athol with his wife Patricia. To Contact him: rflematti@verizon.net or visit his website: rickflemattinaturephotography.com

David W. Flint, lifelong resident and businessman in the Athol-Orange area, has served as River Rat Race chairman since 1991. He is a past president of the Athol Lions Club and founding owner of Flint's Garage Sales since 1978. He has served on the Camp Wiyaka board of directors since 2002 and the Mahar Regional School, Orange, Building Committee and Town of Orange Riverfront Park Committee. He spearheaded fundraising for and construction of the Richard C. Phillips Jr. Pavilion at Silver Lake Park. Flint has been involved in local celebrations including the annual Lion's Club Haunted Hayrides, Starry Starry Night, and Summer Festivals at Athol High School. He has participated in fundraising endeavors. He is a recipient of the Rotary Club's Paul Harris Award, the Knights of Columbus Anchor

Award, and the North Quabbin Chamber of Commerce Citizen of the Year award.

Marcia Gagliardi writes, edits, and publishes at Haley's Antiques and Publishing in Athol, where she buys and sells eclectica of all kinds. In past lives, she was on staff at the *Athol Daily News* and *Patriot-Ledger,* a newspaper serving the South Shore of Boston. She taught English, humanities, and publications in the 1980s at Athol High School and also worked as outreach and special projects coordinator at the Museum of Fine Arts, Boston. She served on North Quabbin nonprofit boards of directors and undertakes civil resistance against nuclear weapons, environmental outrages, and war. She has three adult daughters and their husbands, three grandsons, and a granddaughter. Marcia loves to walk with friends in the North Quabbin woods.

Deborah Leta Habib is co-founder and executive director of Seeds of Solidarity Education Center that she co founded with her husband Ricky Baruc. Seeds of Solidarity is a visionary solar-powered farm and education center based in Orange with a mission to "Awaken the power among youth, schools, and families to Grow Food Everywhere to transform hunger to health and create resilient lives and communities." Deb holds a doctorate in multicultural education from the University of Massachusetts and a masters of science from Antioch New England. She has done undergraduate work in environmental design. She is active on several community boards and among the founders of the North Quabbin Garlic and Arts Festival. Deb is a mother and appreciates the many wonderful friendships she has near and far. She finds refuge in her yoga practice, walks in the forest, and creative pursuits including cooking, pottery, and writing.

Sharon A. Harmon was born in Worcester, Massachusetts and grew up in Worcester and California. She is a poet and freelance writer with 150 published poems and many published stories and articles. She is the poet laureate for Royalston for the 250th Anniversary. Her work has been published in *Chicken Soup for the Soul, Green Living Magazine, Birds & Blooms, A Patchwork Christmas* (2000), and *Swimming With Cats* (2008). She lives deep in the woods of Royalston with her husband Wade and cat Mookie.

Joe Hawkins was executive director of the Athol Area YMCA for forty years. He and his late wife Cindy raised three daughters—Jennifer, Kathryn, and Melissa—all in careers working with children.

Joe was past chair of directors for the Salvation Army and among founders of North Quabbin Community Coalition, Athol Area United Way, and Valuing Our Children. A longtime former member of Athol-Orange Rotary Club, Joe chaired the Human Resource Board for the Town of Orange. Joe received his bachelor's degree from the University of Bridgeport and master's degree from Springfield College. "I am proud to be a resident and active member of this amazing area," Joe said. "People will always support individuals and organizations in need." In order to help address the need for public transportation in North Quabbin rural communities, Joe drives for Community Transit Services. He enjoys every moment with every passenger.

Pat Larson worked for thirty years as an educator in several places including a street academy in South Minneapolis and later public schools in Boston, the Brockton area, and Franklin County. For fourteen years she worked as an educator/organizer and site director in Orange at the North Quabbin Literacy Project. During this time, Pat worked with both teens and adults preparing for the GED and improving basic literacy skills. During the 1990s, Pat worked with students to involve them in projects concerning food and gardening, public transportation, and other issues. Following retirement Pat continued to serve on the Community Transit Services board and volunteer at Athol-Orange Community Television while also working on peace and energy issues through involvement with North Quabbin Energy and the Orange Town Energy Committee. Growing, harvesting, canning, and storing vegetables for winter also keep her busy along with hiking, biking, cross country skiing, and time with family.

Ed Maltby worked with the Adams family to develop a business plan and financing for their new facility and has been general manager of Adams Farm Slaughterhouse LLC since 2009. He is a farmer with more than forty-five years' experience managing conventional and organic dairy, beef, sheep, and vegetable enterprises on farms in Europe and the United States. For the past twenty years, Ed has worked with regional farms to cooperatively convey products into mainstream markets, ranging from direct marketing of lambs and organic produce to establishing a cooperative of dairy farmers. Ed was a founding board member of the Community Involved in Sustaining Agriculture (CISA) and founding member of River Valley Market in Northampton. He serves on the USDA Dairy Industry Advisory Committee to advise the

US Secretary of Agriculture on dairy policy. He serves on the executive committee for the National Organic Coalition.

Michael Mauri makes his living as a licensed forester practicing in the North Quabbin and Connecticut River Valley area. Specializing in forest management over the past twenty years, Mike has always been interested in the stories of people who lived on the land and helped make it what it is today. Old friends camping near a nuclear power plant, thieves stealing firewood, and a notable hayfield are all part of the mix. Mike first became interested in Mary Rowlandson's story while researching a forest management plan for a client in Warwick. Sidetracking into the question, Mike wrote the poem. The Mary Rowlandson poem was first published on Yeoman, a CD of music and poetry recorded by Rob Skelton's Pitchfork with Mike Mauri and released in 2012. It is available at www.cdbaby.com/cd/mikemauri; sample tracks can be heard on SoundCloud at https://soundcloud.com/milelong.

Sean Nolan is a proud Athol native. After spending many years living throughout Massachusetts, he has returned to his beloved home region to raise a family and open a brewery. A graduate of the Siebel Institute of Technology/World Brewing Academy's Brewing Technology program, Sean has worked as a professional brewer at the Cambridge Brewing Company, Idle Hands Craft Ales, and Enlightenment Ales where he was able to hone his craft. Sean's recipes range widely from traditional unfiltered German lagers to Belgian Saisons, to hoppy American beers and Wild ales. Most of his free time is spent wandering the woods of North Quabbin where favorite spots include Royalston Falls, Mount Grace, and Quabbin Gate 37.

Mary-Ann DeVita Palmieri is a resident of New Salem and a forty-year plus newcomer to the North Quabbin area. She and her husband Tony live in a passive solar house that he built in the late seventies. They enjoy all the North Quabbin has to offer, especially its great opportunities to walk and swim and canoe.

Mike Phillips got serious about photography in the early 1980s after he bought a camera from his neighbor. It wasn't long after that he joined the Athol Fire Department as a firefighter and photographer. In 2000, Mike became a freelance photographer for *The Recorder* in Greenfield, where his photos have won awards. In 2006, Mike bought a small boat and has spent countless hours photographing wildlife on the Quabbin Reservoir. He likes walking at different gates of the

Quabbin and photographing its wildlife and history. Gates 29 and 35 are his favorites. Mike has been shooting photos of high school sports for local newspapers for more than fifteen years and submits photos to Athol High School and Mahar Regional School yearbooks each year. Retired and living in Orange, he enjoys woodworking and time with his daughter, granddaughter and friends.

Connie Pike lived in New York City, San Francisco; Oxford, England, and Boston where she met her husband, Mike Magee. The two moved to the North Quabbin in 1990 to the home where Mike was raised. Connie is a psychotherapist in private practice. Also, she owns and teaches at The White Elephant Yoga Studio in Orange.

Deborrah (Boudreau) Porter is a lifelong Atholite (save a couple years residency in beautiful Colorado in the 1970s). She was inspired to write by an Athol High School English teacher, the late Kenneth Ronco, and pursued that dream. She was hired by *Athol Daily News* Editor Barney Cummings in 1987 and worked as a staff reporter and photographer covering a wide variety of assignments throughout the North Quabbin region—from town government meetings to the annual River Rat Race. She was named managing editor in 1992, and in May 2010 following the retirement of Mr. Cummings, was named editor. She is the proud mother of a son, Derek, and resides in Athol in the home built by her grandfather and father. She has been a member of the Athol Lions Club since 1992.

Since 1971, **Phil Rabinowitz** and his wife, Carla, have lived in Royalston where they raised two sons. Phil was a counselor at Greenfield Community College. He was co-founder and executive director of The Literacy Project, an adult basic education program that is the largest provider in western Massachusetts. From 1998 to 2013, he was principal writer for Community Tool Box (ctb.ku.edu), a website at the University of Kansas that is the world's largest collection of information on community capacity building. Phil has served on Royalston town boards, as a board member of the 1794 Meetinghouse, and as chair of the board of Hands Across North Quabbin. He plays guitar and sings with Work in Progress, an eclectic folk band. He sings tenor with Quabbin Valley Pro Musica. He enjoys hiking, biking, and winter sports on the roads and trails in the North Quabbin.

Rise Richardson is director of the Village School in Royalston. Rise grew up in Chicago, graduating with a BA in sociology from the

University of Illinois. She studied with John G. Bennett in England and then settled in Massachusetts. In the 1980s, Rise was part of a group of local parents looking at education to serve the needs of their own children and children in the North Quabbin. They formed the Village School in 1989, which has been a labor of love since. Rise and her husband John also have a small farm in Phillipston with maple sugaring, sheep, hay fields, pastures, woods, and gardens. When Rise is not at the school, you can find her in the summer blissfully weeding in the garden and in the winter, cross-country skiing through the North Quabbin woods. Rise has three grown children, the youngest of whom was lucky enough to be the first Village School graduate.

Photographer **Michael Skillicorn** lives in New Salem. He serves as secretary to the board of the Quabbin Harvest Food Cooperative.

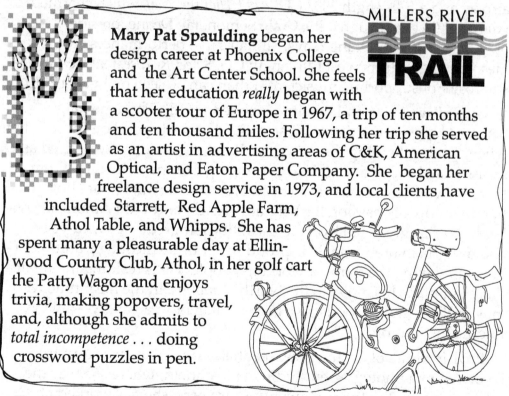

MILLERS RIVER
BLUE
TRAIL

Mary Pat Spaulding began her design career at Phoenix College and the Art Center School. She feels that her education *really* began with a scooter tour of Europe in 1967, a trip of ten months and ten thousand miles. Following her trip she served as an artist in advertising areas of C&K, American Optical, and Eaton Paper Company. She began her freelance design service in 1973, and local clients have included Starrett, Red Apple Farm, Athol Table, and Whipps. She has spent many a pleasurable day at Ellinwood Country Club, Athol, in her golf cart the Patty Wagon and enjoys trivia, making popovers, travel, and, although she admits to *total incompetence . . .* doing crossword puzzles in pen.

Don Stone with his wife Janee has lived, loved, and raised a family on their twenty-five acre homestead in Wendell since 1970. That is, perhaps not long enough to be called native, but it is surely long enough to become deeply rooted and attached to living in the North Quabbin. Don was a professor at the University of Massachusetts for twenty-five years, and for the past twenty years has worked with area small businesses as a business consultant and adviser. He has always enjoyed telling stories, an art form he learned from his father. In addition to his professional writing and research, he enjoys creative writing and has been affiliated with area writers' groups since 1997. He is a part of the North Quabbin Writing Group, which meets twice monthly to share creativity and encouragement. Don welcomes contact with local writers and readers. He can be reached at destone@galaxy.net.

Boston-based recording artist **Ethan Stone** is an Athol native. He performs exclusively where alcohol is not consumed. Since leaving the bar life in 2004, he's worked to stimulate his craft and invest in his community. He created the Tool Town Live concert series and performs at countless alcohol-free benefits throughout the northeast. He has a 2006 single "Too Late" that received international critical acclaim and radio airplay and a full-length 2007 CD, *Ain't That the Way*, which charmed *Worcester Telegram* tough critic Craig Semon. Jay Deane, president of 97.3FM WJDF in Orange says, "Ethan's live performances are mesmerizing." His newest full-length CD, *Sweet Release*, features an all-star roster of supporting musicians. Ethan can be seen on tour in 2015.

Jay Sullivan is from Lowell. A beloved middle child, he long believed he was an artist and a scientist. He made good on those beliefs when, while attending the American Brewers Guild, he was hired as an assistant brewer at Cambridge Brewing Company in 2010. From there he worked his way up to head brewer, a position that allowed him to follow his passion for Belgian, French, and Wild American style beers. He has given talks on the use of local ingredients, wild yeast, and bacteria in brewing. He is proud to continue the long tradition of brewers slaking the thirst of working people. He is residing in Jamaica Plain but plans his move to the North Quabbin. In the meantime, you may find Jay in the woods, in a barrel cellar, or in a gallery—always finding inspiration.

Phyllis Stone of Erving is a Greenfield native. She was formerly co-owner of a photography studio in Greenfield, where she was the office manager. For the past twenty-four years, she has worked at Baystate Franklin Medical Center, Greenfield, where she holds the position of public relations coordinator. She also manages and co-directs a women's a cappella chorus—Clinical Notes—at the hospital. Photography has been Phyllis's hobby for many years. She tends to have a camera on hand whether she's hiking, biking, skiing, kayaking–

or just wandering around town! Most of her bird photos are taken through her living room and dining room windows.

After a career in high-tech, **bg Thurston** lives on a farm in Warwick. Her first book of poetry, *Saving the Lamb* published by Finishing Line Press, was a Massachusetts Book Awards highly recommended reading choice in 2008. Her second book, *Nightwalking*, was released in 2011 by Haley's. bg is writing the history of the 1780s farmhouse she lives in. She teaches poetry workshops year-round, except in March when she is busy with lambing season.

Jonathan von Ranson loves challenge, ideas, and animals, especially dogs and one particular gypsy moth caterpillar he was once amazed to really communicate with. He also loves the living planet that he feels we most enliven when we're at our pared-back, local best. Like his late German-American mechanical engineer father, he likes to build and repair. He was a community newspaperman early in life then turned to homesteading, stonemasonry, and editing from a stone home he and Susan von Ranson built in a remote part of Wendell with their children in the early 1980s. The two of them now live in the center of town in a new, non-electrified home they and much of the town of Wendell worked hard to get approved. It's in one end of an old dairy barn they dismantled before re-erecting it in a big community barnraising.

With her husband Phillip Wiley, **Joyce Wiley** operates Quabbin Skye Vineyard in New Salem.

Casey Williams finds inspiration from things around her every day, everywhere. Patterns on a rusted door, a friend's earring, a scene from a film, a feeling or style of someone's home, dreams, remembering dishes, clothing, or pillows from a relative's house party from 1979, or a towel in her grandmother's bathroom—they all spark ideas and mix together in her mind to produce a collection of work ranging from large acrylic abstract paintings to small, delicate illustrations plus decorative handmades. Casey produced a series of small folk-art paintings of the nine towns in the North Quabbin, where she grew up and where she lives. In her own artistic way, she has set out to stamp the North Quabbin as a noteworthy area. She hopes viewers will enjoy her work purely as object, purely for the look" and "feel of it. She hopes they will have relatable connections of their own.

Ed the Wizard moved to the Pioneer Valley area in 1977 to attend UMass Amherst. Soon he moved to New Salem and worked as a cook in area restaurants before joining the US Air Force. Ed returned and made the North Quabbin his permanent home and trained as a toolmaker . Skilled with his hands and with an artistic eye, Ed left the tool trade and taught himself to be a woodcarver of marine wildlife art and signs; many of his signs are still to be seen the North Quabbin area. In 1998 after he read *Harry Potter and the Sorcerer's Stone,* Ed rekindled his childhood love of magic. Inspired by the character Headmaster Albus Dumbledore, Ed taught himself the art of prestidigitation. By 2015, Ed the Wizard could be found performing his unique style of magic all across the Northeast.

Mark Wright was born and raised in Athol and spent much of his youth exploring the back roads and woods of the North Quabbin. He spent many days fishing, hiking, and traveling unmarked dirt roads with his parents and extended family. Summer weekends most always included a fresh rainbow trout lunch. A graduate of Athol High School, Wright went on to earn degrees in business, psychology, and theology. His career experience includes arbitrage, personnel management, artistic production design, and event management. His work has taken him across the country and internationally, and he has called Boston, South Florida, New York, and Austin home at times. Having returned to his roots in the North Quabbin, he is Executive Director of the North Quabbin Chamber of Commerce & Visitors Bureau. He spends personal time playing and composing music, hiking, exploring the culinary arts, becoming a better oenophile, and being with Lilyana.

Allen Young, who holds a master's degree from the Columbia University Graduate School of Journalism, left a reporter's position at the *Washington Post* in 1967 at age twenty-six to become involved in the anti-war underground press. He later became a gay activist/journalist, then moved to Royalston as part of the back-to-the-land movement. He was a reporter and assistant editor for the *Athol Daily News* and later director of community relations for Athol Memorial Hospital. His photo-illustrated book, *North of Quabbin Revisited,* published by Haley's in 2003, describes the region in great detail. His most recent book— his fourteenth, *The Man Who Got Lost* also published by Haley's—is a collection of his articles from the *Athol Daily News*. His column, "Inside/Outside," appears weekly in the newspaper, and he is writing a memoir.

Leigh Youngblood is the executive director of Mount Grace Land Conservation Trust, a regional land trust with a staff of twelve, nationally recognized for its innovative and collaborative accomplishments. Leigh's childhood was spent in diverse landscapes from the inner city of Springfield to the coral reefs of Oahu, the Arizona desert, and most impressionably, the western foothills of the Sierra Nevada. With family roots in the Ozark Mountains and rural New England, arriving for work in the North Quabbin in 1994, Leigh felt immediately at home. An intermittent decade in the Wendell Writer's Workshop introduced her to the wonders of writing. A proud mother who recently became a grandmother, Leigh remarried in 2014 and lives in Warwick with her husband Michael Humphries.

Phil Zahodiakin is a freelance journalist living in Orange. He was previously a Washington, DC, reporter covering energy and environmental issues at the agencies, Capitol Hill, and the courts. He is also a freelance book reviewer, for *Kirkus Indie* and previously for *Publishers Weekly*. "North Quabbin Shadows" is his first published poem.

photo by Marcia Gagliardi

Keystone Bridge, built in 1866, spans New Salem's Swift River near Gate 30 in the Quabbin Reservation. Gate 30 and the Keystone Bridge serve as a fitting gateway to the North Quabbin.

CPSIA information can be obtained
at www.ICGtesting.com
Printed in the USA
FSOW04n1207041117
40638FS